Depeche Mode

FAITH AND DEVOTION

First published in 2019 by
Palazzo Editions Ltd
15 Church Road
London, SW13 9HE
www.palazzoeditions.com

Design and layout copyright
© 2018 Palazzo Editions Ltd
Text © 2018 Ian Gittins

A CIP catalogue record for this
book is available from the
British Library.

ISBN 978-1-78675-064-8

Manufactured in China

10 9 8 7 6 5 4 3 2 1

Designed by Becky Clarke
for Palazzo Editions

RIGHT Martin Gore and Depeche
Mode performing live at the
O2 Arena in Prague on the
Tour of the Universe tour,
14th January 2010.

PAGE 4 Martin Gore, Andrew
Fletcher and Dave Gahan, 2001

Depeche Mode

FAITH AND DEVOTION

IAN GITTINS

PALAZZO

Contents

INTRODUCTION

Outsider Art

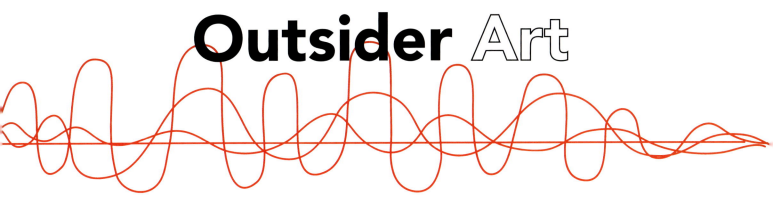

The post-punk era of the early 1980s was one of the most fertile in British music history. Famously, it was a time that enabled some truly unlikely outsiders, liberated by punk's DIY ethic, to grab guitars and synthesizers and plant their New Wave freak flags on the summit of the charts.

It was a brief, blessed age when dreamers, visionaries, and chancers could weave provocative spells with newly affordable electronic instruments. The most innovative artists self-identified as futurists, and for a heady few years, they appeared to be inventing it.

The Human League, Gary Numan, Soft Cell, Heaven 17, New Order, ABC, Spandau Ballet, Orchestral Manoeuvres in the Dark, (early, pre-bluster) Simple Minds . . . they were provincial plotters and arch art-terrorists on a mission to subvert; a quest to craft perfect pop. Most of them are now long gone or reduced to ploughing a sorry furrow on rock's nostalgia circuit.

Only one of this original gaggle of electro-alchemists has gone on, forty years later, to become leather-trousered, swaggering musical colossi, rock and roll A-listers capable of routinely filling sports stadiums all around the globe. Only one group cleaved hard to their singular, transgressional musical ethos and conquered the world with it.

They are Depeche Mode, and their rise to superstardom is one of the most extraordinary tales in modern pop history.

In their early years, Depeche Mode were never cool. They came from a bland, dreary new town in

the middle of nowhere, widely regarded as typifying provincial obscurity. They utterly lacked the art-school backgrounds and pretensions of their showier peers; right up until their first hit single, two of them worked in a bank.

Depeche Mode were never "The Band Most Likely To." Shy and awkward, they weren't in the vanguard of the synth-poppers with a manifesto looking to tear up the rules of chart-pop and the music industry. Initially, indeed, their chirpy, spindly ditties were roundly mocked by Britain's tastemakers and critical arbiters of hip.

Nor were their infant years easy ones. In the immediate wake of the surprise success of their 1981 debut album, *Speak & Spell*, band leader and main songwriter Vince Clarke abruptly quit the group to pursue alternative projects. It was a body blow that few bands would survive, but Depeche Mode did more than that. They prospered.

Discovering a phenomenally talented second songwriter in their ranks in quiet-man keyboardist Martin Gore, the group slowly but surely shifted their musical focus from Clarke's lightweight, positivist-pop to something with far more heft and gravitas: something immeasurably *darker*.

Blessed with the velvet croon and million-watt charisma of front man Dave Gahan, one of life's natural rock stars, Depeche Mode began to hew out their own singular strain of electro-driven, rock-tinged pop noir. The tunes seduced, but the lyrical themes remained resolutely, obsessively deep: sex, religion, corruption, venality, betrayal.

They were a band to inspire devotion, and it duly followed. Having crossed over from cult status to

Not yet swaggering musical colossi: Depeche Mode, Basildon

mainstream success in their native UK by the end of the 1980s, they soon saw America follow suit. With "Personal Jesus" on MTV and FM radio heavy rotation, the gargantuan 1990 album *Violator* was to shift more than three million copies in the US alone.

It was a triumph remarkable for the fact that Depeche Mode had achieved it without shearing off any of their experimental edges or toning down any of their brooding lyrical fixations—and yet it came at a heavy price. Megastar status does not suit everybody, and the band members who had always been prone to rock star excess went into precipitous, potentially fatal personal spirals.

Gahan's meltdown was the most public and spectacular. Addicted to cocaine and heroin, the singer suffered an onstage drug-linked heart attack in 1993, attempted suicide two years later, and overdosed in Los Angeles's Sunset Marquis in 1996. Meanwhile, behind the scenes, the private Gore was battling alcoholism as fellow founding member Andrew Fletcher fought crippling depression.

Depeche Mode should have gone down in flames, many times, but somehow this most resilient band did what they have always done: they survived, even crafting compelling, cathartic, and multi-million-selling albums such as *Songs of Faith and Devotion* and *Ultra* from the depths of personal despair.

Today, four decades on from their first stirrings, Depeche Mode are long cleaned-up and sober, yet continue to make albums that are far edgier and more challenging than is appropriate for a band so long in the tooth. Their 2017 album, *Spirit*, with its unexpectedly ferocious commentary on global politics, was one of their most powerful and lauded in years.

They emerged from nowhere and willed into being a rock stardom that very nearly killed them—but which somehow ended up making them stronger. This is the precarious, extraordinary story of Depeche Mode.

Dave Gahan models rock star excess, Molson Canadian Amphitheatre, September 2013

1
THE WALLS
OF BASILDON

Some places will just never be cool. Across the globe there are towns and cities that, through geographical location, economic makeup, or sheer bad luck, seem destined to be natural laughing-stocks: hapless punchlines to cruel jokes at their own expense.

In the US, the image of comedian W. C. Fields's hometown never quite recovered from his tart assertion that his gravestone epitaph should read: "All in all, I'd rather be in Philadelphia." In Germany, people laugh at Stuttgart. Britain's second-largest city, Birmingham, is resigned to being depicted as a particularly charmless concrete jungle.

Deservedly or not, from the outside these unlucky locales are regarded as being prosaic, parochial, and utterly devoid of romance or glamour—sterile, culture-free zones of suffocating banality.

Which brings us to Basildon.

Depeche Mode's hometown is nobody's idea of a vibrant, agenda-setting metropolis. Thirty miles east of London in the solidly working-class county of Essex, itself the butt of a fair few jokes over the years, Basildon was designated a "New Town" in 1949 and built largely to serve as a commuter town for the capital.

The UK government also gave generous grants to companies such as Ford and GEC-Marconi to set up bases in the town. This sudden spurt of industrial growth, some decidedly ugly, hyper-functional town-center architecture, and a perceived lack of history and character led to a general snobbish disdain towards the town.

No, Basildon would never be cool, and was not a place you could even imagine anything cool coming from . . . until Depeche Mode did.

The band's creative mainstay, Martin Gore, was not born in Basildon but transplanted there. Born Martin Lee Gore in nearby Dagenham on July 23, 1961, he was only a toddler when his parents, engineer/driver Dave and care home worker Pamela, moved to the new town.

The infant Gore was, by his own account, a shy and self-contained child, hardworking and low-profile at school. At the age of five he went through an unfortunate phase of "beating up other children," which was ended by a furious lecture from his dad: "I'm glad I got such a talking to. It made me very passive and harmless."

PREVIOUS PAGE Andrew Fletcher, Dave Gahan, Vince Clarke and Martin Gore, 1980

LEFT Who could ever call Basildon boring?

Gore's main passion at school was for languages, until he developed a burgeoning interest in music when he was around ten. Seduced by his mum's old Elvis and Chuck Berry 45s, he was also excited by the glitzy chart-pop of the day, his favorite being the since-disgraced glam rock icon, Gary Glitter.

"I nearly joined his fan club," he divulged, years later. "The glamour of early 1970s pop appealed . . .

I hunted high and low for his version of 'Baby Please Don't Go.' It's terrible, but it made me want to be a pop star."

The newly musically inclined Gore attempted to learn to play the oboe, violin, and piano at Nicholas Comprehensive School in Basildon before his mother gave him an acoustic guitar when he was thirteen. She also gave him some bombshell news about his origins.

Pamela told her son that her husband, and the man who had raised him, was not his biological father. Gore was shocked, but naturally continued to regard his loving male guardian, Dave Gore, as his true dad.

Throwing himself into guitar, Gore began learning basic chords. He even started writing rudimentary songs, although his shyness left him unable—or, at least, unwilling—to play them to anybody.

This introverted nature also meant that he had little social life in his teens. However, for a while, he did have a girlfriend: Anne Swindell, who had previously

dated another Nicholas Comprehensive pupil—one Andrew Fletcher.

Born in Nottingham on July 8, 1961, Fletcher had, like Gore, moved to Basildon as an infant when his engineer father had changed jobs. "It was a job for a house," he was to tell Stephen Dalton in a wide-ranging interview for *Uncut* magazine in 2001. "If you could get a job, you could get a house."

At the age of eight, Fletcher—who appears to have been known as "Fletch" since his very earliest school days—joined a local branch of a Christian youth organization, the Boys' Brigade. Although he initially signed up so he could play for their football team, he soon became devoutly religious.

Regarding himself as a born-again Christian, the young Fletcher took to attending church seven days a week—as did another Boys' Brigade attendee and Nicholas Comprehensive pupil, Vince Martin.

Born in the north-east London suburb of South Woodford on July 3, 1960, Martin had, like Gore and Fletcher, moved to Basildon at a very early age. An awkward, twitchy child, in his late pre-teens he embraced Christianity as wholeheartedly as Fletcher.

"Me and Vince were into the preaching side—trying to convert non-believers," Fletcher was to confess to *NME* in 1983. "Vince was number three in the local hierarchy."

It was music that was to lead Vince Martin away from the Church. At eleven, he joined a local Saturday morning music school. There, incidentally, his path crossed with another Nicholas Comprehensive pupil, an effervescent young female singer named Alison Moyet.

"I never spoke to [Vince], but I remember him because he and his two brothers all had white-blond hair," Moyet told the *Independent* in 2008. "They looked like a family of ducks."

After a brief, Gore-like flirtation with the oboe, Vince Martin turned to the acoustic guitar, motivated by an early-teenage infatuation with Simon & Garfunkel. With Christian friends, he formed a short-lived folk-gospel group.

In 1977, as punk exploded, came a two-man band, No Romance in China, with Vince on guitar and vocals and Fletcher on bass. Their repertoire, according to Steve Malins in his authoritative *Depeche Mode:*

A Biography, first consisted of covers of the Everly Brothers and Gerry and the Pacemakers.

However, the duo quickly updated their influences. "No Romance In China tried to be like The Cure," Fletch confessed to *Number One* magazine in 1985. "We were into their *Three Imaginary Boys* LP. Vince used to attempt to sing like Robert Smith."

No Romance in China failed to emulate The Cure's meteoric rise and split in 1979. In the same year, Fletcher and Gore left school after taking their A levels. Gore's linguistic skills showed as he passed in French and German.

He failed his Maths A level, however, which arguably made his next decision somewhat questionable: he went to work in a bank.

"[After A levels] I had to make a decision about the future, which shocked me greatly," he confessed a few years later. "I didn't have the necessary motivation to do much, like going to university. I didn't want to leave school. I felt secure there."

LEFT Now-disgraced glam rocker Gary Glitter excited a young Gore

RIGHT Alison Moyet: "Vince looks like a duck"

Fletcher also decided against further education, and followed his friend into the financial sector. He took a job at Sun Life Insurance in the City of London, just down the road from where Gore worked as a cashier in a NatWest Bank.

However, Gore had also formed a band. With an old school friend, Philip Burdett, he became a duo named Norman & The Worms who specialized in folk-tinged covers, apparently including a novel take on the theme from Australian kids' TV series *Skippy the Bush Kangaroo*.

Meanwhile, Vince hooked up with another Basildon friend and Nicholas alumnus, Perry Bamonte, in a group called The Plan. It was short-lived (although Bamonte was to go on to greater things, as a keyboardist and guitarist with The Cure).

The band merry-go-round continued as Vince reunited with Fletcher in a group called Composition of Sound. They played occasionally at a Basildon pub called the Van Gogh, as did both Norman & The Worms and Alison Moyet's punk-influenced band, The Vandals.

It would likely have remained a minor, inconsequential scene, had not Martin Gore made a game-changing move. After saving up £300 from his NatWest wages, he bought a Moog Prodigy synthesizer.

Vince was in the audience when Gore's keyboards made their debut at a Norman & The Worms gig and was highly impressed: "Martin came along with a synth, which I thought was brilliant. Here was an instrument that didn't need its own amp—you could just plug it into the PA!"

Vince and Fletcher invited Gore—or, rather, his precious keyboard—to join Composition of Sound. The initial line-up had Gore on synth, Fletcher on bass, and Vince on guitar and vocals. However, Vince, who was nearly as self-conscious as Gore, had no desire to be a front man.

Gore was by now also playing his Moog in another band, The French Look, fronted by a Basildon face called Rob Marlow. These groups all hung out together and rehearsed at the Woodlands Youth Club at a local school; a place which was to be the scene of a crucial encounter.

Composition of Sound and The French Look were rehearsing in two adjacent rooms at Woodlands

LEFT Art Garfunkel & Paul Simon: an unlikely influence on Vince Martin

BELOW "Heroes" was Dave Gahan's unwitting audition for the band

"I didn't have the necessary motivation to do much, like going to university."

GORE

"HEROES" DAVID BOWIE   AYL1-3857

Previously released as AFL1-2522

when Vince heard the latter band's soundman, a local tattooed hustler named Dave Gahan, belting out a surprisingly tuneful version of David Bowie's "Heroes" through the wall.

A light bulb went on in Vince's head. Could this be Composition of Sound's missing piece—and his own escape route from singing duties?

It could, and it was—but Dave Gahan was made of very different stuff from Martin Gore, Andy Fletcher, or Vince Martin.

Gahan was born David Callcott in Epping, Essex, on May 9, 1962. His part-Malaysian father, Len Callcott, and his mother, Sylvia, worked on London buses, as a driver and conductor respectively. He was only six months old when his parents split and his dad left the family.

He was still only a toddler when he moved with his mother and older sister, Sue, to Basildon, after Sylvia married her second husband, Jack Gahan, an oil company office worker. Just like Gore, the young Gahan grew up assuming the man he called "Dad" was his biological father.

This illusion was smashed when Jack Gahan died in 1972, and Gahan came home shortly afterwards to find Len Callcott in the house. Sylvia informed her son that this was his father. Bursting into tears, Gahan argued with her: *How could he be? His dad was dead!*

Callcott became an occasional presence in his son's life for the following year, until he again vanished off the radar. Sylvia told Gahan that he had moved to Jersey to open a hotel.

Possibly triggered by this seismic personal upheaval, the young Gahan rapidly went off the rails. An irregular attendee at Barstable School in Basildon, he became a teenage delinquent who appeared in juvenile court for spray-painting graffiti, vandalism, and joyriding.

"I just wanted attention," he told *Uncut* in 2001. "I put my mum through a rough time. It was petty crap—driving and taking away, criminal damage, theft.

"I was pretty wild. I loved the excitement of nicking a motor, screeching off and being chased by the police. Hiding behind a wall with your heart

beating gives you a real kick—will they get you?"

Tattooed by fourteen, experimenting with soft drugs, and getting trains to London to go clubbing, Gahan left school at sixteen with few qualifications. He worked his way through "about 20" menial jobs, including laboring on building sites, selling soft drinks, and working as a cashier in a gas station.

Concerned that his life was going nowhere, he applied for a job as an apprentice fitter with North Thames Gas. His probation officer advised him to come clean about his criminal record at the interview. When he consequently failed to get the job, he trashed the probation office. This landed Gahan in a juvenile delinquent attendance center in Romford, where he was obliged to spend every weekend for a year.

"It was a real pain in the arse," he later reminisced. "You had to work—I remember doing boxing, stuff like that. You had to have your hair cut. I was told very clearly that my next thing was detention centre."

Gahan hauled himself a little nearer to the straight and narrow when he enrolled in Southend Technical College at seventeen, gaining a certificate in shop window dressing. He also discovered music.

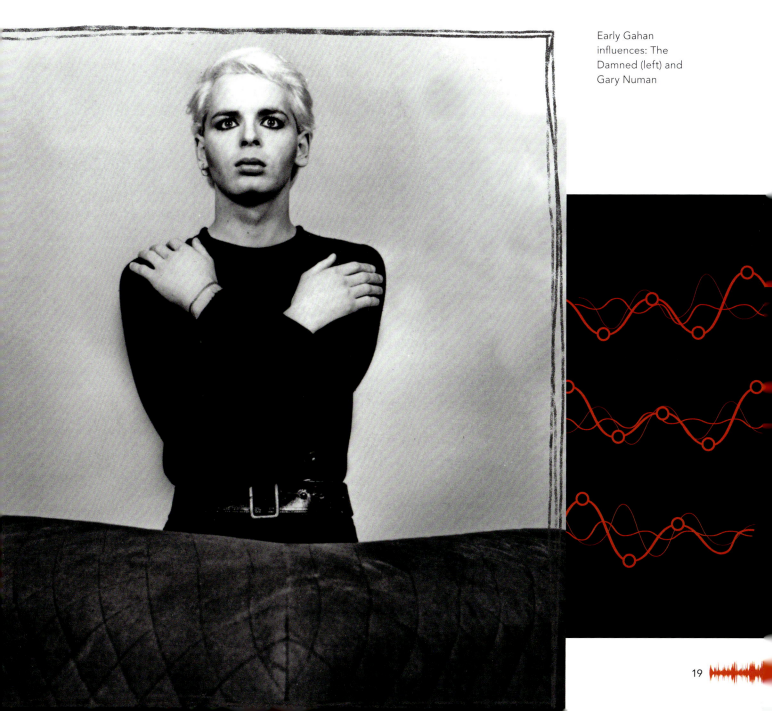

Early Gahan influences: The Damned (left) and Gary Numan

"I was pretty wild.
I loved the excitement of
nicking a motor, screeching
off and being chased by
the police."

GAHAN

> ## "Vince was the boss of the band. He was unbelievably driven."
>
> **FLETCHER**

Compared to the more reserved Gore, Fletcher, and Martin, Gahan had been a punk rock early adopter, joining The Damned's fan club and pogoing to The Clash, 999, and X-Ray Spex in Chelmsford. Also intrigued by electronic music, he followed Gary Numan around the UK on his 1979 breakthrough tour.

So, Gahan was a streetwise, roguish wild spirit, a college student also working part-time as a window dresser, when Vince asked him to join Composition of Sound in 1980. His first gig with them came when they supported Martin Gore's other band, The French Look, at the youth club at their old alma mater, Nicholas Comprehensive.

Gahan was an immediate hit, his rich baritone and innate sense of showmanship a welcome counterpoint to his more withdrawn new bandmates (it was a better night for Composition of Sound than for The French Look, who argued onstage and split up).

With Gahan now *in situ*, Vince Martin was delighted to be relieved of the front man duties that had always sat awkwardly with him. He celebrated this new freedom by adopting a stage name. There again, it wasn't exactly Ziggy Stardust: from now on, he would be known as Vince Clarke.

New moniker or not, there was no doubt that Clarke was the driving force of Composition of Sound. He and Gore had both been writing songs since they were about twelve, but the diffident Gore was more than happy to let Clarke shape the group's musical vision.

It was a vision that didn't include Fletcher's bass or Clarke's guitar. Excited by breakthrough electronic artists such as Numan, Human League, and, especially, Orchestral Manoeuvres in the Dark, Clarke decreed that Composition of Sound would be a synthesizer-only group.

Fletcher bought a keyboard with his Sun Life salary, while Clarke scraped together the pennies from a part-time job working in a local yoghurt factory to buy a Kawai synth. "It was about £125, I think, maybe even £200," he told Jonathan Miller in the biography *Stripped: Depeche Mode.* "God knows where I got the money from! I saved hard."

Fletcher corroborated this account in a 2009 BBC TV documentary, *Synth Britannia*: "Vince was the boss of the band. He was unbelievably driven. He used to earn £30 a week at a yoghurt factory and save up £27.70 of that to buy a new synth."

They had the synths; now they needed songs. Composition of Sound began evening and weekend rehearsals, firstly in Clarke's parents' garage, then in Woodlands Youth Centre, before a local vicar allowed them to use a storage room in his church. Maybe it was their karmic reward for Clarke and Fletch's earlier devout churchgoing.

Newly motivated by OMD and Tubeway Army scoring chart hits, Clarke insisted the band discard most of the halting, half-formed song scraps they had written to date and compose brand new material. He quickly became the band's main songwriter.

Some early Composition of Sound tracks which never made it as far as the recording process included "Reason Man," "Tomorrow's Dance," and "Addiction ." However, one song which did survive, and which marked their baby steps into the wider world, was "Photographic."

A Clarke composition, "Photographic" opened with stabs of staccato, frenetic one-fingered synth, before a more luscious electronic beat kicked in. For its part, Gahan's atypically soft vocal seemed both to echo Gary Numan's detached, alien delivery ("I. Take. Pictures.") and anticipate the camp melodrama of Soft Cell's Marc Almond.

"Photographic" was the clear standout when Composition of Sound ventured out from the church storage room for occasional gigs, including one at a Southend bikers' pub called the Alexandra. It was

The shock of the new, 1980s style: the Human League (left) and Orchestral Manoeuvres in the Dark

Futurists? New Romantics? Soft Cell (left) and Spandau Ballet (above)

RIGHT Boy George (right) with friend and minor popstar Marilyn

also the lead track on a three-song demo tape they sent out to various venues and promoters.

This scored them a handful of gigs, including at the Bridge House, a hard rock pub in east London's Canning Town. Composition of Sound played a few Wednesday nights to the proverbial two men and a dog.

"They came walking in like four office boys who've just got their first job," the former Bridge House owner, Terry Murphy, reminisced to Trevor Baker in his book *Depeche Mode: The Early Years*. "They were very shy [when they played]. Dave used to be terrified."

More tellingly, the demo tape also secured them a Saturday night residency at Croc's, a nightclub in Rayleigh, just eight miles down the road from Basildon. Crocs was at least on nodding terms with a major musical scene then developing in the capital.

Taking its lead from the ever-changing, peacock-hued futurism of David Bowie, London's fledgling, electropop-based New Romantic scene was unfolding around clubs such as Club for Heroes and Blitz, and painted-faces about town like Boy George and Spandau Ballet. Gahan had visited them once or twice.

Croc's was a kind of Essex outpost for fledgling New Romantics: Gary and Martin Kemp had been known to visit, and Culture Club were to play their first ever gig there. It was also where Composition of

Sound came to the attention of another very driven London scenester.

By the age of sixteen, Stevo Pearce had left school with no qualifications and was playing cutting-edge, heavy-duty electronic music at a DJ residency at the Chelsea Drugstore on the King's Road. Regarded as a tastemaker of electropop and industrial music, he began compiling a "Futurist chart" for weekly UK music paper *Sounds*.

With characteristic contrariness, Stevo hated the term "Futurist"—"It became linked with Visage and all that, which made it a bit of a joke," he said in *Depeche Mode: A Biography*—but liked some of the demo tapes he received at *Sounds*. He decided to self-release a compilation album that he would call *Some Bizzare*: the name that he would later bestow upon his independent record label.

Having seen an early Composition of Sound gig at Croc's, Stevo wanted them on this sampler album. However, the band were already engaged in their own campaign to try to scare up record-label interest.

Scraping together £50 to hire a studio in Barking, east London, for a day, the group recorded a demo tape. Rather than sending copies in the post, they fixed on the audacious strategy of delivering them to record companies in person.

Of course, this meant they got to experience the joys of rejection at first hand. Dave Gahan claims that on one fateful day the band were turned away from no fewer than twelve record labels before finishing up at west London post-punk independent mecca, Rough Trade Records.

"We were all dressed up in our Futurist gear, and stuff," Vince Clarke told Jonathan Miller in *Stripped*. "The nicest people were at Rough Trade: they were prepared to sit and listen to the tape."

Rough Trade liked the demo but Composition of Sound weren't their sort of band, and so they pointed them towards a tyro independent music mogul who happened to be in the building at the same time.

His name was Daniel Miller.

> "We were all dressed up in our Futurist gear, and stuff. The nicest people were at Rough Trade: they were prepared to sit and listen to the tape."
>
> **CLARKE**

RIGHT Vince Clarke, 1984.
FAR RIGHT A fresh-faced Dave Gahan
BELOW "How do you turn it on?"

2
ARRIVAL &
DEPARTURE

aniel Otto Junius Miller's music career to date had been decidedly idiosyncratic. A film student at Guildford School of Art at the end of the 1960s, he had grown bored with rock music, turning instead to the experimental electronica of German groups such as Can, Faust, Neu! and, later, Kraftwerk.

After a spell DJ'ing in Switzerland, Miller returned to London during the punk rock maelstrom. Excited by both the music and, primarily, the anyone-can-do-it attitude that underpinned it, he resolved to make music himself.

Buying a relatively cheap Korg 700S synthesizer, Miller recorded two blasts of minimal, attitudinal fuzzy electronica on a reel-to-reel tape recorder: "T.V.O.D." and "Warm Leatherette." Giving himself the name The Normal, he distributed them through Rough Trade record shops, dubbing his label Mute Records.

The support of late-night Radio 1 DJ John Peel, press coverage, and word of mouth made the single a cult hit. Together with a Scottish electronic musician, Robert Rental, Miller went on tour as Robert Rental & The Normal, supporting Belfast punks Stiff Little Fingers.

Despite having no long-term plan for Mute Records beyond the Normal single, Miller had included a label address on the sleeve and returned home from the tour to a slew of demo tapes. Interest piqued, he

„the normal"

PREVIOUS PAGE Depeche Mode, 1981

LEFT Not yet pop poseurs

RIGHT "You call this Normal?"

LEFT Early Mute artists DAF (Deutsch-Amerikanische Freundschaft)

RIGHT Goodbye Composition of Sound! Hello Depeche Mode!

began releasing avant-garde electronica singles by the likes of Fad Gadget and Deutsch Amerikanische Freundschaft (D.A.F.).

Miller and Fad Gadget, aka Frank Tovey, also formed a conceptual, virtual band named Silicon Teens, pretending it was a four-piece teenage all-synthesizer group. Their 1980 Mute album, *Music for Parties*, largely featured synth-pop covers of hoary old rock classics such as "Memphis, Tennessee" and "Oh Boy!"

"I thought that if I was head of EMI, that's what I'd pay a million pounds for right now—a two-boy, two-girl electronic pop group," Miller later told *NME*. "So, I made one up."

The twenty-nine-year-old Miller was at this stage an electropop evangelist, as disdainful of guitars and conventional rock-music instrumentation as was Vince Clarke. When he was introduced to Composition of Sound during his visit to Rough Trade, and invited to listen to their demo tape, it should have been a meeting of minds. It wasn't.

"[Daniel] took one look at us, went 'Yuk!,' walked out and slammed the door," Dave Gahan would later recall to *Sounds*. Vince Clarke has the same memory: "Daniel only listened for about five seconds and then said, 'No!,'" he told Jonathan Miller in *Stripped*.

Miller's own memories of the encounter are less dramatic. "[On that day] I had some technical problem

"[Daniel] took one look at us, went 'Yuk!,' walked out and slammed the door."

GAHAN

with a Fad Gadget sleeve," he said. "I just looked at [Composition of Sound] and thought, 'I don't need to listen to this stuff right now,' and went off to do whatever it was that I had to do."

Undeterred by this setback, Composition of Sound ploughed on, writing and rehearsing new tracks and paying their live dues with regular gigs at the Bridge House. As a live act, they were decidedly low-maintenance. With no guitars, drums, or amps to transport, the band could simply tuck their keyboards

under their arms and go to gigs on the Tube. Gore and Fletcher would travel from their bank jobs in their suits, changing into their showier stage clothes at the venue.

It was around this time that Composition of Sound made a major and significant decision: they ceased trading as Composition of Sound.

Dave Gahan, in particular, had never greatly cared for the clunky moniker, and suggested they appropriate the name of a French style magazine: *Depeche Mode* (the phrase is often mistranslated as "Fast Fashion," but means something more akin to "Fashion Telegram"). It seemed he was keeping the "French Look" theme going.

No stranger to a name change himself, band leader Vince Clarke was up for the idea: "We just liked the sound of the words," he reflected, years later. So, that was it. Depeche Mode it was.

As interest in the band slowly grew, they played a more prestigious London gig at Ronnie Scott's legendary jazz club in Soho. Yet it was at Canning

Town's rough and ready Bridge House, on November 11, 1980, that they were to cross paths again with both Stevo and Daniel Miller.

A committed fan of the band, Stevo was still bending their ear asking them to appear on his imminent *Some Bizzare* compilation and sign to his label. Daniel Miller, meanwhile, was at the venue to see the headline act, Fad Gadget.

"Fad Gadget had just finished a sound check and normally I would have gone off with them, but for some reason I stayed behind and watched this group who looked like a dodgy New Romantic band," he told Steve Malins in *Depeche Mode: A Biography*.

"I hated the New Romantics but what came out of the speakers was incredible. I thought, 'Well, everybody plays a good song first'—but it just got better and better."

Miller did not initially even recognize Depeche Mode as the band he had brusquely dismissed at Rough Trade, but he warmed to their youth and innate tunefulness. He speculated that they could even be a real-life incarnation of his virtual electropop naïfs, the Silicon Teens.

Heading backstage after their set, Miller told the band that he liked them and wanted to release a single by them on Mute Records.

"There was some sort of conversation, probably, where I said, 'You could be a really big pop band. I think what you're doing is fantastic: it's really new, but it's still pop,'" he told Jonathan Miller in *Stripped*.

Miller went on to say that Mute had never had a big pop hit but they would like to try with Depeche. The fledgling band were flattered, as well as impressed that the indie label boss was proposing putting out a single on a trial basis, with no formal contract.

After months of music industry rejection, Depeche were suddenly the subject of a low-level indie label bidding war, with Stevo still also keen to work with them. However, this particular conflict was resolved extremely amicably.

LEFT Stevo's *Some Bizzare* album

RIGHT The The's Matt Johnson, not cracking an uncertain smile

"I walked backstage at one of those early gigs and said to Daniel, 'I just told Depeche Mode that you're a lovely guy and they should go with you," Stevo told Steve Malins in *Depeche Mode: A Biography*. "I told them that Daniel was very honest and trustworthy."

In this spirit of cooperation, Miller was willing not only for the band to contribute "Photographic" to Stevo's *Some Bizzare* album, but to produce the track himself. He did so in a studio in London's East End at the end of 1980.

At this stage, Depeche Mode's musical equipment consisted of three cheap synths and a low-rent drum machine. Miller brought along his own ARP 2600 synth, and recalls Clarke being blown away by its analog sequencer function that allowed musicians to program in notes rather than play them live.

"Vince was mesmerised by it, and so the ARP became crucial to the early development of Depeche Mode," Miller said in *Stripped*. "They immediately got into it."

> **"I hated the New Romantics but what came out of the speakers was incredible. I thought, 'Well, everybody plays a good song first'– but it just got better and better."**
>
> MILLER

With the ARP's sequencer to the fore, Depeche quickly recorded "Photographic" for the *Some Bizzare* compilation, which was released in February 1981. They were in very good company.

Stevo's sampler showcased three other future chart stars in (then ethereal, later cheesy) synth-pop duo Blancmange, the cerebral yet visceral The The, and Soft Cell's queasy, querulous "The Girl with the Patent Leather Face." It also piqued the interest of the UK music press.

Chris Bohn in *NME* appreciated Depeche's "very assured, neatly structured" offering. *New Sounds New Styles* magazine talked to them, noting that their track was by far the most upbeat on the sampler. "Vince doesn't write gloomy songs," Dave Gahan sweetly explained.

Indeed, at this stage their guileless positivity was Depeche Mode's main attraction for Daniel Miller, who was still half-entertaining the notion that they could be the Silicon Teens made flesh. Yet siren voices began to attempt to try to lure the group away from Mute.

At the dawn of the eighties, major labels were looking to snaffle up any electronic group that appeared even vaguely linked to the emergent New Romantic electropop scene. The media focus on the *Some Bizzare* album brought Depeche Mode to their attention.

> ## "Deadpan vocals, programmed rhythm rejoinders and a candyfloss melody make for a pleasant three minutes."
>
> **CHRIS BOHN,** *NME*

BELOW Gore and Gahan, not giving up the day jobs

RIGHT Depeche had a 1981 Valentine's Day date with Ultravox

There were meetings and even offers of head-turning amounts of money, but having made their decision, Depeche Mode stuck with Mute, with Vince Clarke telling *Sounds*: "We've got a better chance [there] . . . Daniel had success with the Silicon Teens and we've got the same sort of lightweight feeling to us."

Yet if things now seemed to be moving fast for Depeche Mode, their feet remained firmly on the ground. Gahan was still a student and window dresser; the cautious Gore and Fletcher were holding down their banking day jobs. The driven Vince Clarke remained the band's motor—including writing their debut Mute single.

In December 1980, the group went into Blackwing Studios, a complex housed in a former church in Southwark, south London. Ever the muso, Clarke

was excited to be in a 16-track studio. With Daniel Miller again producing, they set about recording "Dreaming of Me" and its B-side, "Ice Machine."

Clarke spent most of the two-day session in the studio, picking up tips and know-how from Miller. The other band members joined them in the evenings, with Gore and Fletcher getting the Tube over from their nearby office jobs.

The circumstances of its creation may have been dully pragmatic, but "Dreaming of Me" certainly wasn't. From its opening robotic drum beat and tinny synth doodle, it was a delight, with Gahan's rich growl surfing a sparse but seductive melody.

The slightly lesser "Ice Machine" harbored a similar nifty, nebulous charm. It was the first hint that Depeche Mode could be something special—even if they were still awkwardly, gawkily, feeling their way.

A buzz was growing. On Valentine's Day 1981, Depeche played the Rainbow Theatre, which electropop scenesters and promoters Steve Strange and Rusty Egan had for one night renamed "The People's Palace." They supported Ultravox, then at No. 2 in the singles chart with "Vienna."

A week later, Mute released "Dreaming of Me," which was lauded in equivocal terms by their impressed-despite-himself champion on *NME*, Chris Bohn. Calling it "sweetly unassuming electronic whimsy," he concluded: "Deadpan vocals, programmed rhythm rejoinders and a candyfloss melody make for a pleasant three minutes."

More pertinently, the single also got played on BBC Radio 1's evening alternative-music shows—

and scored some consequent chart action. Four weeks after its release, it broke into the UK's Top 75 at No. 57.

Nothing excites the record industry like a hit. On a flying visit to the UK, the larger-than-life Seymour Stein, the head of Sire Records who had signed Talking Heads, the Ramones, and the Pretenders to the US major and was about to discover Madonna, bumped into Daniel Miller on a visit to Rough Trade.

Stein was looking for new talent and Miller suggested Depeche Mode. The exec hugely impressed the band by meeting them not in a swanky West End boardroom but at a gig at Sweeney's Disco in Basildon.

"We didn't even have a dressing room," Fletcher later marveled. "We had to meet him on the stairway. He signed us from our first single."

Indeed, having previously licensed Daniel Miller's The Normal single and Fad Gadget for the US, Stein was excited by Depeche Mode's potential and signed them up for America. Now there was just the small matter of making an album.

Over the summer of 1981, in between occasional gigs, Depeche set about recording their debut at Blackwing. With Gore and Fletcher still wage slaves at their banks, and Gahan studying in Southend, their day-to-day work routine remained unaltered.

"I would be at Blackwing in the day to give Vince a bit of advice on how to get sounds and help him with the technology," Miller recalled to Steve Malins. "Then Fletch and Mart arrived after work in dodgy suits and would be far more interested in eating their takeaways and playing the games machine."

Yet this routine suited Clarke. A natural loner who was not without control freak tendencies, he was happy working alone translating his growing arsenal of songs to synths and sequencers. And luckily for Depeche Mode, he was coming up with gold dust.

Pert, perky, and perfectly formed, Clarke's song-doodles began to coalesce into a spirited, upbeat album of positivist electropop—and the next missive from it was to confirm just how huge they could be.

Depeche's second Mute single, "New Life," was a quantum leap from its predecessor. A gossamer trifle, lighter than air, it unfolded around a twitchy, truly irresistible synth riff with an indefinable urgency. It sounded like a song that Radio 1 would play to death.

It was. In June, in the same week that Depeche did a session for Radio 1 DJ Richard Skinner's evening show (oddly neglecting to play their new single),

"Then Fletch and Mart arrived after work in dodgy suits and would be far more interested in eating their takeaways and playing the games machine."

MILLER

ABOVE Vince Clarke at a pool party, 1981
LEFT Sack the stylist!

"New Life" was released and went straight into the chart. Four weeks later it had soared to No. 11.

This breakthrough led to Depeche Mode undergoing a rite of passage faced by any British pop band on the up—a first appearance on *Top of the Pops*. As usual, they went on public transport, synths under their arms.

In leather trousers, bullet belts, and, in Fletcher's case, a biker's cap, the band mimed their way through the tune as a nervous Gahan gyrated. They were still teenagers and suddenly they were pop stars. With "New Life," Depeche Mode had arrived—but what was it *about*?

The answer, apparently, was nothing at all: "Vince's songs are odd because they don't mean anything," Martin Gore confessed to one interviewer. "He looks for a melody, then finds words that rhyme."

To his dubious credit, Clarke has never disputed this analysis: "There were no messages in the songs at all—nothing!" he told Jonathan Miller in *Stripped*. "They were very stupid lyrics, you know?"

Stupid or not, "New Life" beguiled enough pop fans to rack up more than half a million sales during its fifteen-week stay in the UK chart. By the time it dropped out, Gore and Fletcher were finally sufficiently convinced of Depeche Mode's future prospects to give up their day jobs.

The pair handed in their notices at Sun Life and the NatWest. Dave Gahan also quit his art course in Southend and his window dressing work—the latter after beating a hasty retreat when one West End department store where he worked was mobbed by female fans who spotted him in the window.

Just six months after gawping at their first sequencer, Depeche Mode were suddenly full-time, bona fide chart-pop stars—and the hits kept coming. Released in September, "Just Can't Get Enough," another intoxicating Vince Clarke bauble, charted even higher than "New Life," penetrating the Top 10 and coming to rest at No. 8.

It was all stoking anticipation for their debut album, and when it came, on October 5, *Speak & Spell* was an intriguing proposition. Wrapped in a dreadful, cryptic cover image of a swan in a plastic bag, it was an efficient object lesson in what Vince Clarke had taken to calling "U.P."—"Ultrapop."

Taking Ultrapop on to *Top of The Pops*, 1981

ARRIVAL & DEPARTURE 43

"Bubbly and brief,
like the best pop should be."

RECORD MIRROR

Speak & Spell

TRACK LIST

SIDE ONE
New Life
I Sometimes Wish I Was Dead
Puppets
Boys Say Go!
Nodisco
What's Your Name?

SIDE TWO
Photographic
Tora! Tora! Tora!
Big Muff
Any Second Now (Voices)
Just Can't Get Enough

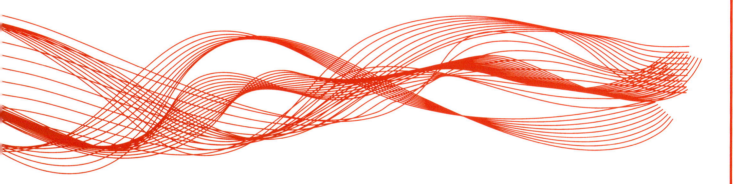

Recorded at Blackwing Studios, London, England

Produced by Daniel Miller & Depeche Mode

Personnel
Dave Gahan: lead vocals
Martin Gore: keyboards, backing vocals, lead vocals on "Any Second Now (Voices)"
Andy Fletcher: keyboards, backing vocals
Vince Clarke: keyboards, drum machine, backing vocals, guitar

Cover art
Brian Griffin: photography

Released 5 Oct 1981

Label Mute STUMM 5

Highest chart position on release
UK 10, GER 49, SWE 21, US 192

Notes
When the album was first released on cassette back in 1981 in the then-Yugoslavia, the track "I Sometimes Wish I Was Dead" was completely missing. This mistake was later noticed and there was an approx. 500 copy reissue made, this time including the track. The early tapes with one less track are now well sought after.

The singles and "Photographic" were the obvious standouts but the album throbbed with a sweet, melodic intensity, not least the jittery, Human League-esque "Boys Say Go!" Only a pair of Martin Gore-written tracks, "Tora! Tora! Tora!" and the questionably titled instrumental "Big Muff," introduced a mildly more portentous tone.

It was cheery, if hardly challenging, and UK reviewers treated it accordingly. *Sounds* dubbed it a "perfectly uncontrived pop soufflé"; *Melody Maker* lauded it as "clearly sparkling with new life." For *Record Mirror*, it was "bubbly and brief, like the best pop should be."

While these notices were favorable, they tended to paint Depeche Mode as skilled but ultimately inconsequential. Yet, writing in *NME*, the most influential music journalist of the day, Paul Morley, divined purpose and profundity beneath the surface perkiness.

Praising their "generous, silly, susceptible electro-tickled pop," he speculated that "Depeche Mode, apparently, could move . . . far up and away from constructing slightly sarcastic jingles," and arrived at a dubious conclusion, given Clarke's self-confessed "very stupid" lyrics: "Depeche Mode introduce literacy into bubblegum."

Critical approval was fine but Depeche Mode were a pop group: from the very outset, they had been adamant that what they wanted was to have hits. They were to get their wish. On its release, *Speak & Spell* sailed up the album chart to No. 10.

It was a remarkable success and it should have heralded the happiest of times for the band. But something was very wrong in paradise.

A creature of the studio and a pop craftsman, Vince Clarke had little time for the ephemera that came with fame. For him, the interviews and promotional duties that accompanied releasing records were an irritant, a distraction to drag him away from his precious keyboards and sequencer.

This attitude put him firmly at odds with the rest of Depeche Mode, whose early, kids-in-a-sweetshop reaction to success meant that they were willing to jump through any hoops that journalists and photographers might hold up. Pull zany faces for *Smash Hits*? Sure, whatever!

The nadir of Clarke's distaste for such fripperies came when Depeche encountered the *Daily Star*'s pop hack, Rick Sky, who asked whether it was an advantage for a pop star to be good-looking. "Obviously, it's an advantage in *life* to be good-looking," Clarke replied.

When the downmarket tabloid appeared, his words had been badly twisted to read: "Ugly bands don't get anywhere in this business." Horrified by this misquotation, Clarke reportedly refused to leave his home for days.

Declining future media duties, Clarke seemed to resent the fact that Gahan, Gore, and Fletcher were willing to go on playing the game and appeared blithely indifferent to the perfidies of the press. As the band's driving force brooded, a split began to open up in the group.

This problem was evident to Daniel Miller when he went out to join the group on a debut mini-tour of Europe, just prior to the release of *Speak & Spell*. "A rift was growing between Vince and the other members of the band," he recalled to Steve Malins. "It got to the point where they weren't talking to each other."

This rift was to become a chasm. When the group returned to the UK and to Basildon, Clarke visited each other member's house in turn to tell them that he had had enough. He was leaving the band.

Clarke attempted to reduce the impact of the blow. He stressed that he did not want to leave the group in the lurch: if they wanted, he would play with them on the imminent UK tour to promote *Speak & Spell*, and announce his departure when it was over.

In truth, his decision came as no shock to the rest of the band. Clarke had been a brooding, angst-ridden presence for weeks, particularly since the *Daily Star* incident. He had hardly exchanged a word with his bandmates on the European tour.

"Depeche Mode introduce literacy into bubblegum."

PAUL MORLEY, *NME*

> # "He just felt that we were becoming public property, he didn't like what was happening to Depeche Mode, didn't like being famous and didn't like touring."
>
> **FLETCHER**

"The general atmosphere had been getting really bad," Fletcher told Steve Malins. "It was like us three, and Vince on his own. He just felt that we were becoming public property, he didn't like what was happening to Depeche Mode, didn't like being famous and didn't like touring."

Nevertheless, this was a major blow. Depeche weren't just losing a band member: from the outset, Vince Clarke had been their glue and their motor, their leader and, crucially, their chief songwriter. Many groups would have crumbled after such a setback.

In particular, the naturally cautious Gore and Fletcher could have been forgiven for panicking, having only just finally surrendered their secure nine-to-five lifestyles to commit fully to the band. So, would they put in calls to the NatWest and Sun Life, begging for their jobs back?

They didn't. They had had a taste of the pop star life and did not want to give it up. Instead, they resolved on a new division of duties. Fletcher would take on much of the admin and management duties of the band Clarke had previously handled. Gore would become the main songwriter.

"No one thought about the band splitting up," Daniel Miller was to confirm, years later. "Everybody close to them knew that Martin was a really good songwriter. Even on Vince's tracks, his melodic contributions were very good."

"I think Vince was maybe a bit surprised at how we reacted [to his departure]," Dave Gahan told *Sounds* in 1982. "But we were fairly prepared."

Three weeks after the release of *Speak & Spell*, Depeche began their UK tour, supported by Blancmange, with Clarke still *in situ*. With fans not knowing it was his swansong with the band, it could have made for a tense tour bus atmosphere, but the members were later to report that they remained cordial on the road.

Onstage, Depeche Mode still looked a work in progress. Their image, a mix of leather, frills, and chain-store flash, was uncoordinated, to say the least: the three-synth setup and Clarke, Gore, and Fletcher's shyness was underwhelming. The saving grace was the charismatic Gahan, who was beginning to develop into a compelling front man.

Yet they were, noted Barney Hoskyns of *NME*, ". . . received with nothing short of rapture. A companion made the observation that one doesn't so much dance to Depeche Mode as respond/flinch to the direct stimulus of their machines."

The tour ended in mid-November with two nights at the Lyceum in London. A slightly tardy two weeks later (were they hoping for a late change of heart?), Mute officially announced that Vince Clarke had left the group.

The press statement painted the breakup as an amicable affair, claiming that Vince remained open to writing for or collaborating with Depeche Mode in the future. The remaining band members were possibly unconvinced by this line of thought.

"It wasn't amicable at all," Dave Gahan was to confess, years later. "There was a lot of bad feeling on both parts. It was about a year before it finally died down, and until then it was pretty vile."

Clarke was gone and Depeche Mode, still an infant band finding their feet, had to forge a new identity without the man seen as their brains, heart, and soul. It was an intimidating task that, from the outside, looked to verge on the impossible.

With hindsight, the extraordinary thing is just how phlegmatically the remaining members soldiered on.

"Looking back, I think we should have been slightly more worried than we were," conceded Martin Gore, years later. "When your chief songwriter leaves the band, you should worry a bit!

"I suppose that is one of the good things about being young . . . if we had panicked, we probably wouldn't be here today."

And then there were three . . . the post-Vince Mode

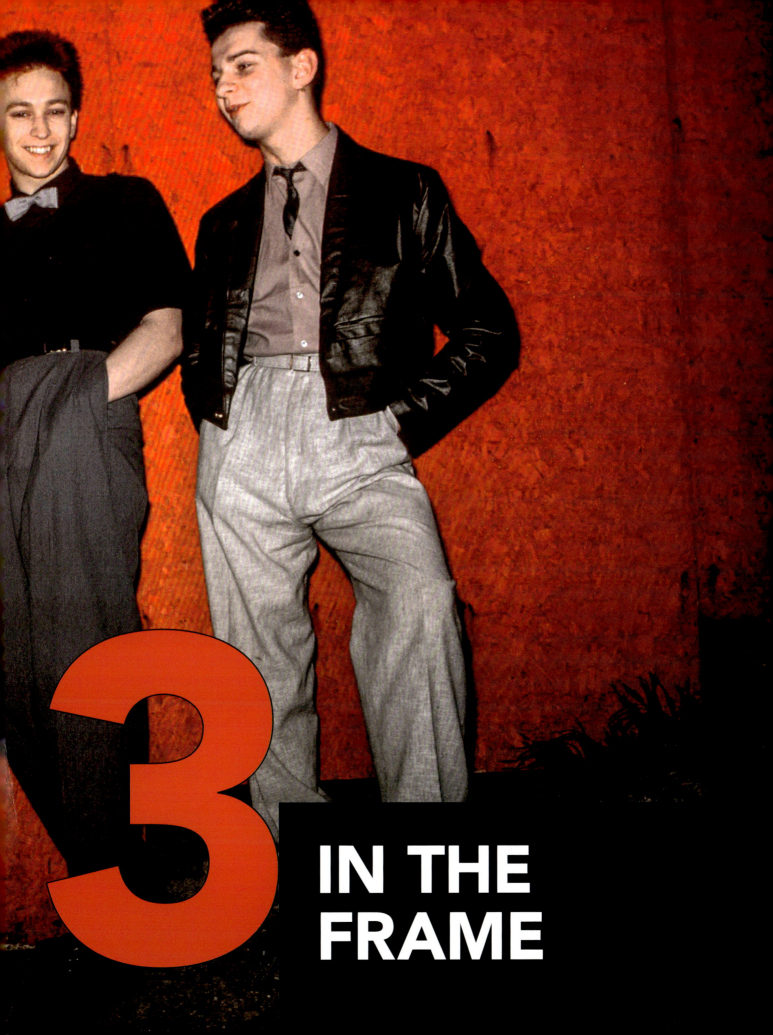

3

IN THE FRAME

Depeche Mode had no time to hang around. Their first ever trip to America was looming large on the horizon.

Less than two months after Vince Clarke's departure was announced, the band were due to play two nights in New York in January, at Seymour Stein's instigation, to help pave the way for the US release of *Speak & Spell*. They knew they had to fill that Vince-sized hole onstage—and fast.

Gahan, Gore, and Fletcher placed a small ad in the back of *Melody Maker*, the traditional port of call for UK bands in search of musical reinforcements. It was short, and to the point:

NAME BAND REQUIRE SYNTHESIZER PLAYER MUST BE UNDER 21

The advert attracted a fair number of applicants, many of whom had likely seen the news story in the same issue of *Melody Maker*, about Vince Clarke quitting Depeche Mode, and had put two and two together. Depeche auditioned dozens of hopefuls, many of whom had the New Romantic dress sense down pat but were sorely lacking in musicianship.

One applicant, however, seemed to be far more what they wanted.

Born in Hammersmith, west London, on June 1, 1959, Alan Charles Wilder had ignored the advert's chief stipulation, already being the ripe old age of twenty-two-and-a-half. His background was also notably different to that of the three Basildon boys.

The youngest of three sons in a distinctly middle-class family, Wilder was musically gifted, learning piano and flute and joining the brass band and orchestra at his grammar school in Shepherd's Bush. He was to achieve grade 8—the top level—in piano.

Yet despite this talent, Wilder was not overly interested in school in general, passing only three O levels. He went into the sixth form to study A levels

but lost interest and dropped out after just one year, dismaying his parents by choosing instead to live off unemployment benefits.

Unlike his elder brothers, both classically trained musicians whose interests lay in Bach and Mozart, Wilder had been inducted into the thrill of pop music by the wham-bam glam rock of Marc Bolan and David Bowie. He knew from his early teens that he wanted to work in music.

Initially, this was easier said than done: "After I left school in 1975, I was unemployed all the time," he told Steve Malins in *Depeche Mode: A Biography*. "My parents advised me to apply to recording studios. I think I got rejected about forty times."

Application number 41 had led to a job as a tape operator, or tape op—the bottom of the recording-studio food chain—at DJM Studios in New Oxford Street, central London. Wilder learned his way around studio tech, met proper pop stars the Rubettes, and resolved to be a musician.

His musical career since then had been both eventful and a bit of a non-event. Meeting a soft-rock band called the Dragons at DJM, he joined them as keyboardist and moved to Bristol, where they were based. The Dragons released a single, "Misbehavin'," and supported the Damned at one show, but then disbanded.

Returning to London, Wilder adopted the stage name Alan Normal to join a New Wave/power pop band called Dafne and the Tenderspots. Next had come a white reggae band, Real to Real, followed by a nondescript rock band named the Hitmen.

The Hitmen had just split when Wilder saw Depeche Mode's small ad in *Melody Maker*. He hoped his keyboard skills might compensate for his lack of knowledge of their genre (and, of course, his age). Having first been vetted by Daniel Miller, at his

"My parents advised me to apply to recording studios. I think I got rejected about forty times."

WILDER

audition he was surprised by the rudimentary level of the group's musical skills.

"Before I joined Depeche Mode, I didn't know the first thing about electronic music," he admitted to Steve Malins. "But I could play along with *them* immediately."

Wilder's musicianship—and lack of reverence towards them—was immediately appreciated by Depeche, who had tired of trying out star-struck fans who couldn't play. Even so, the keyboardist was later to describe this first meeting as "tricky."

"I'm sort of middle class and they were working-class lads," he told Malins. "Musically, I thought they were a bit naïve-sounding, but there was something interesting about it—and I was sort of in a desperate situation where I'd take just about any gig at the time."

Wilder initially found Gahan, Gore, and Fletcher to be painfully shy (as well as wearing Marks & Spencer jumpers) and wasn't even all that fond of their tunes, but he liked them and was perfectly content when they said they weren't looking for a full-time band

member but they wanted him to play keyboards on tour with them.

And they still didn't know that he was twenty-two-and-a-half.

Wilder was thus not required when, for the first time since Clarke's departure, Depeche Mode went back into Blackwing Studio in late November 1981 to record a new single. With nobody else in the band at this point having any pretensions of being songwriters, it was down to Martin Gore to carve a path forward.

He did so by going back to the past. The germs of the single "See You" lay in a song he had written back in his teenage acoustic duo, Norman & The Worms. Yet in Blackwing, under the watchful producer's eye of Daniel Miller, it became something else entirely.

"Martin came up with this song and it was very basic, just a melody on a Casio synth and Martin tapping the beat with his foot," Miller was to recall. "The song was all there, but in terms of arrangement and sound there was no indication of which way to go.

"It was very different to Vince, who'd had a much stronger sense of what he wanted, but the

atmosphere in the studio was very exciting and quite positive."

Gore had recently invested some of his royalty money in a PPG Wave 2, a relatively expensive analog/digital hybrid German synthesizer. By the normal primitive standards of Depeche's equipment, it was a cutting-edge piece of kit that allowed Gore to modify and sequence multiple notes and tones.

Applying this slick technology to Norman & The Worms' acoustic original, Gore came up with a lustrous gem. "See You" was bright as a button, a febrile synth shimmer underpinning a pristine melody, with lyrics that seemed to represent a tentative step on from the inanities of *Speak & Spell*.

"The middle-eight goes: '*Well, I know five years is a long time and that times change/But I think that you'll find people are basically the same,*'" Gore explained to *New Sounds, New Styles*, analyzing his ditty about trying to rekindle a lost love.

"It's good—serious, but funny. I like it because those words aren't used much in songs. It's just the things people say."

If Gore's explanation was a little gauche and naïve, then so were the lyrics—but at least he was thinking about them, which was in itself a step on from Vince Clarke's disinterested approach.

Alan Wilder played his first show with Depeche Mode at their old stomping ground of Croc's in Rayleigh at the start of 1982. A couple of days later, the band took their first flight to the US to play the Ritz in New York City on January 22 and 23.

The trip was not an unqualified success. Invited to play "See You" on *Top of the Pops* the night before they flew out, Daniel Miller made sure the group could fulfill both commitments by splashing out Mute's money to book them onto Concorde.

The supersonic flight was a thrill but inevitably meant Depeche were jet-lagged and disoriented for

"Depeche Mode utilizes commercial song formulas with almost unerring precision."

TROUSER PRESS

LEFT Depeche Mode hit New York, January 1982
RIGHT Jet-lagged and disoriented?

the NY shows, a disadvantage that was compounded by onstage equipment failures. Yet both New York shows were packed and well received, even if hip US music magazine *Trouser Press*, a largely Anglophile publication that routinely lauded the likes of The Cure, was ambivalent.

"Depeche Mode utilizes commercial song formulas with almost unerring precision," their reviewer noted. "Three minutes at a time can be enjoyable: more forces you to come to terms with their limitations. A simple, predictable sonic palette (synth only) heightens the difficulty."

Yet if Depeche were yet to crack the States, Britain's pop kids were fast growing to love them. Released on their return, "See You" quickly became their biggest hit to date, coming to rest at No. 6 in the singles chart as the band set off on a UK tour.

However, the song had a rival for radio play and chart success—an extremely familiar face from Depeche Mode's very recent history.

Having quit the band just weeks earlier, the workaholic Vince Clarke had been predictably busy,

"I think we were kind of jealous to be honest. The first song [Yazoo] had out, 'Only You,' was a song he tried to give us. I was like 'I don't think so.' And then, of course, it was a huge hit."

GAHAN

purchasing yet more synthesizers and a sequencer and writing new tracks at home. He had come up with a mellifluous, melancholic little number called "Only You."

True to his word on leaving the band, Clarke initially offered the song to Depeche but the group knocked it back, feeling it was too similar to other offerings out there. Undeterred, their former leader looked elsewhere.

Clarke reconnected with another face on Basildon's music scene, former punk singer Alison Moyet from the nearby town of Billericay, who loved "Only You" and gave it another dimension with her soulful croon. The duo took the name Yazoo, and Daniel Miller released the single on Mute in April.

Sales were initially underwhelming, but "Only You" scraped into the lower reaches of the chart, hung in there and then gained traction. Inexorably climbing, it came to a halt at No. 2, only kept off the top by Eurovision Song Contest winner Nicole's mawkish "A Little Peace."

Depeche Mode's See You tour had by now moved through Europe to the States, where they were playing eight dates (during which Dave Gahan had an arm in a sling from having tattoos removed). Thousands of miles from home, they were still more than aware of their ex-bandmate's triumph—especially as their own latest offering was not doing so well.

Another Martin Gore composition, their fifth single, "The Meaning of Love," was pretty but decidedly lightweight and no advance on "See You." Ending their sequence of every British single surpassing the one before, it stalled in the chart at No. 12.

It all began an unspoken but intense Mute rivalry between Depeche Mode and Vince Clarke that was to last for many years, even after both parties ascended to stratospheric heights.

LEFT Yazoo: "We've got a massive hit!"
BELOW Depeche Mode: "Oh."

"There was rivalry, and I wanted to be fair to everybody," Daniel Miller confessed in *Depeche Mode: A Biography*. "Depeche Mode were making great records, and so were Yazoo."

"Although there were problems, neither side made it an impossible situation. No one said, 'Well, if he's going to be on the label, we're going to leave,' or anything like that. It was never *quite* that bitchy."

"I think we were kind of jealous, to be honest," Dave Gahan was to confess, many years later, to *Rolling Stone*. "The first song [Yazoo] had out, 'Only You,' was a song he tried to give us. I was like, 'I don't think so.' And then, of course, it was a huge hit."

The undoubted tensions between the two parties were exacerbated by the fact that Yazoo's vivacious follow-up, "Don't Go," was in the top three of the UK singles chart when Depeche Mode went into Blackwing Studio in July 1982 to begin work on their second album.

Or, rather, most of them did.

Easily the most musically adept of their number, and having toured with Depeche around the UK, Europe, and US (and even by now confessed his true age), Alan Wilder hoped to be involved in making the record. It was not to be. He had been hired as a live band member and, for now, that was exactly what he would be staying.

"When the second LP came to be made, I'd done my bit and I thought I warranted involvement," he recalled to *Uncut* magazine in 2001. "I had something to contribute. They said no." (Although the rest of the band never told him this in person—hating confrontation, they deputed Daniel Miller to do so.)

"The problem was that they had something to prove to themselves. The three of them didn't want the press to say they'd just roped in a musician to make things easier after Vince left. I was pretty upset, and there was ill-feeling from me about that."

Wilder's consternation was understandable, and yet so was Gore, Gahan, and Fletcher's wariness. Previously, they had become used to being viewed as mere decorative adjuncts to Vince Clarke's

"We were floundering around, not knowing where to go. It was a real mishmash."

GORE

musical vision and creative genius. His control and micromanagement could be intimidating.

"Vince always wanted to do a lot in the studio, and the rest of us would feel restricted," Fletcher was to tell *New Sounds, New Styles*. "If we had an idea, we'd feel frightened to say anything."

"No, not frightened," Gahan corrected him gently in the interview. "We were *uncomfortable*."

The original members thus hated the idea of being seen as clinging to new member Wilder's coattails as if he were Vince 2.0. They knew they had to stand on their own two feet—even if it would not be an easy process.

Martin Gore's songwriting was very much a work in progress. Having shown himself adept at melody, he was nonetheless green when it came to the nuts and bolts of the composition process. Luckily, the band's label boss and *de facto* producer had faith in him.

"I just thought, 'Well, let's get on with the next record,'" Daniel Miller was to tell *Sound on Sound* magazine. "I knew Martin could write songs."

Gore had big shoes to fill and his first steps were tentative. Whereas Clarke had always turned up in the studio with near-finished songs on demos, his successor would arrive with little more than an idea for a melody and the vague shape of a tune.

"We don't make elaborate preparation with music and lyrics before going into the studio," he told *ZigZag* magazine. "Usually we have a loose framework to build upon."

The raw material that Gore was bringing into Blackwing varied greatly. The singles "See You" and "The Meaning of Love" had been an obvious continuation of Vince Clarke's "Ultrapop": chart-friendly ditties that Gore later confessed were "really poppy stuff [that] I felt we had to do, because that's what we were doing on the last record."

Yet even at this early stage, it was becoming evident that Gore's own songwriting instincts were far darker and more experimental than Clarke's *Smash Hits*-friendly trifles. Typical was the track that was to open the album and be their next single, "Leave in Silence."

A moody, ambient musing on ending a ruined relationship that was "*spreading like a cancer*," "Leave in Silence" was a brooding affair, all hurt glances and hidden spiritual bruises. Despite Gahan's atypically fey vocal, it had emotional heft, even if its relatively muted chorus hardly suited daytime Radio 1.

This was to prove a drawback. Released on August 16, the elegiac "Leave in Silence" only reached No. 18 in the chart, markedly lower than Yazoo were achieving, and Depeche's worst-performing single since their debut. It did, however, serve as an accurate harbinger for the album that was to follow.

Released the following month, *A Broken Frame* was a decidedly mixed bag. Ambient, downbeat murmurs such as "My Secret Garden" and "Monument" rubbed shoulders with effervescent pop nuggets like "A Photograph of You." It was, as Gore was later to acknowledge, all over the shop.

"We were floundering around, not knowing where to go," he told *Kingsize* magazine in 2001. "It was a real mishmash. Some tracks were old, among the first things I'd written, and others I came up with on the spot."

One of the record's biggest flaws was that it failed to take advantage of Dave Gahan's rich, redolent baritone. Its nervy songs required him to deliver his vocal in a hushed, coy whisper: on tracks such as the parping "Satellite" he seemed to be apologizing for being there.

A Broken Frame was a halting, contradictory, uneven album, and its fault lines were noted by critics. In *Smash Hits*, band supporter Pete Silverton worried that the album betrayed a lack of purpose but ended up rooting for what he called its "tinkly-bonk whimsy."

Sounds and *Record Mirror* compared *A Broken Frame* unfavorably to Yazoo's almost simultaneously released debut, *Upstairs at Eric's*. *Melody Maker* did the same, acknowledging a degree of musical development but concluding that Depeche were "essentially vacuous."

In the studio, Depeche were resolutely still a trio

"At times it reaches high points far exceeding their first album."

NOISE!

A Broken Frame

TRACK LIST

SIDE ONE
Leave in Silence

My Secret Garden

Monument

Nothing to Fear

See You

SIDE TWO
Satellite

The Meaning of Love

A Photograph of You

Shouldn't Have Done That

The Sun & The Rainfall

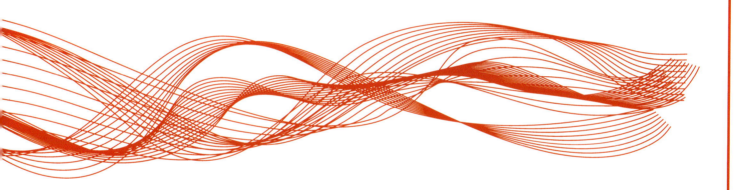

Recorded at Blackwing Studios, London, England

Produced by Daniel Miller & Depeche Mode

Personnel
Dave Gahan: lead vocals
Martin Gore: keyboards, programming, backing and lead vocals
Andy Fletcher: keyboards, backing vocals

Cover art
Brian Griffin: photography
Martyn Atkins: design
Ching Ching Lee: calligraphy

Released 27 Sept 1982

Label Mute STUMM 9

Highest chart position on release
UK 8, SWE 22, GER 56, US 177

Notes
In 2015, the Greek synthpop duo Marsheaux released a complete cover version of *A Broken Frame* on Undo Records. The reviewer for *Release* magazine wrote that this version was not "anything essential" but well done.

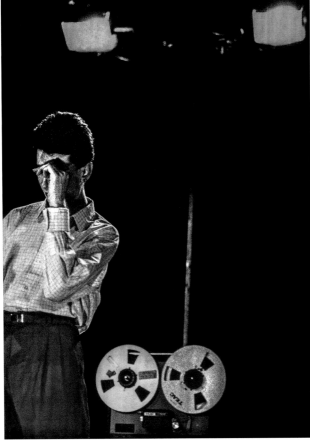

With the passing of time, Andy Fletcher was also clear-eyed about its plus and minus points: "The newer songs tended to be a bit darker and the older songs were more innocent and poppy. I suppose it was an album of getting to grips with Vince not being there, but it had some good tunes on it."

A Broken Frame was a distinctly imperfect document but even in those early days Depeche Mode were beginning to inspire the fierce loyalty that would come to define their fan base. Its chart peak of No. 8 was two places higher than that attained by *Speak & Spell*.

On its release, the band toured the UK. Still provincial boys at heart, Gore, Gahan, and Fletcher took their partners on the road with them, as the girls had been getting a little unhappy about the levels of interest in their boyfriends from female fans.

Slogging between dates, with a night off a rarity, Depeche Mode were learning a lesson—even intense, arty would-be futurists had to pay their dues.

"I'll never forget those first tours," Andrew Fletcher reflected to the *Daily Telegraph* in 1995. "We were crammed into a van along with our equipment and driving for what seemed like years along motorways."

Such straitened circumstances can nurture togetherness or hostility, and luckily for Depeche, it was proving to be the former. The venues and crowds were getting notably bigger than previous jaunts, with two sold-out nights at London's Hammersmith Odeon, and the original members were getting on well with the easy-going Wilder.

This amity continued when the *A Broken Frame* tour switched to Europe, with no dates in France but ten in Germany, where the band were already picking up a hardcore following. Depeche Mode were growing fast—including, formally, from a trio to a quartet.

Their fan club newsletter broke the news: "Alan Wilder is now a permanent member of Depeche Mode . . . although he didn't play on the last three hit singles or *A Broken Frame*, he will be joining Dave, Martin and Andy in the studio from now on."

So, they didn't mind him being that critical year older, after all. Yet it said a lot about the band's awkward, self-conscious nature in those days that, even cooped up in a tour van for weeks, they couldn't ask their new colleague face-to-face if he would go full-time.

"Daniel Miller phoned me [to tell him]," Wilder laughed to Steve Malins in *Depeche Mode: A Biography*. "I think the band found it difficult to be the bearers of good news, as well as bad . . ."

Some publications were kinder: "What can be appreciated is their quickening concision, their increasing artfulness, [and] Martin Gore's impressive songs," noted *NME*. Dave Henderson, in *Noise!* magazine, also struck a positive note: "At times it reaches high points far exceeding their first album."

Martin Gore's high-pressure emergence as a songwriter had been no disgrace, then, but ultimately *A Broken Frame* was a mixed bag of an album; an awkward transition between what Depeche Mode had been and what they were to become.

It was a stepping-stone, and one that Depeche Mode were later to describe as a wobbly one: "I don't think our second album was a masterpiece," Gore said in 2001. "We just about got away with it."

Speaking to *Melody Maker* in 1990, Dave Gahan was even more dismissive: "I think we all feel that *A Broken Frame* is, in retrospect, our weakest album. Definitely. It's very, very patchy.

"We were learning at that point. It was very naïve. It was Martin's first album as a songwriter . . . he was thrown in at the deep end, to be honest."

LEFT Dave Gahan on stage in Rotterdam, 1982

ABOVE "Look what it says in *Suosikki* magazine!"

"The newer songs tended to be a bit darker and the older songs were more innocent and poppy."

FLETCHER

Photobooth larks, platform posing and a wrong number,
Hounslow Station, 1982

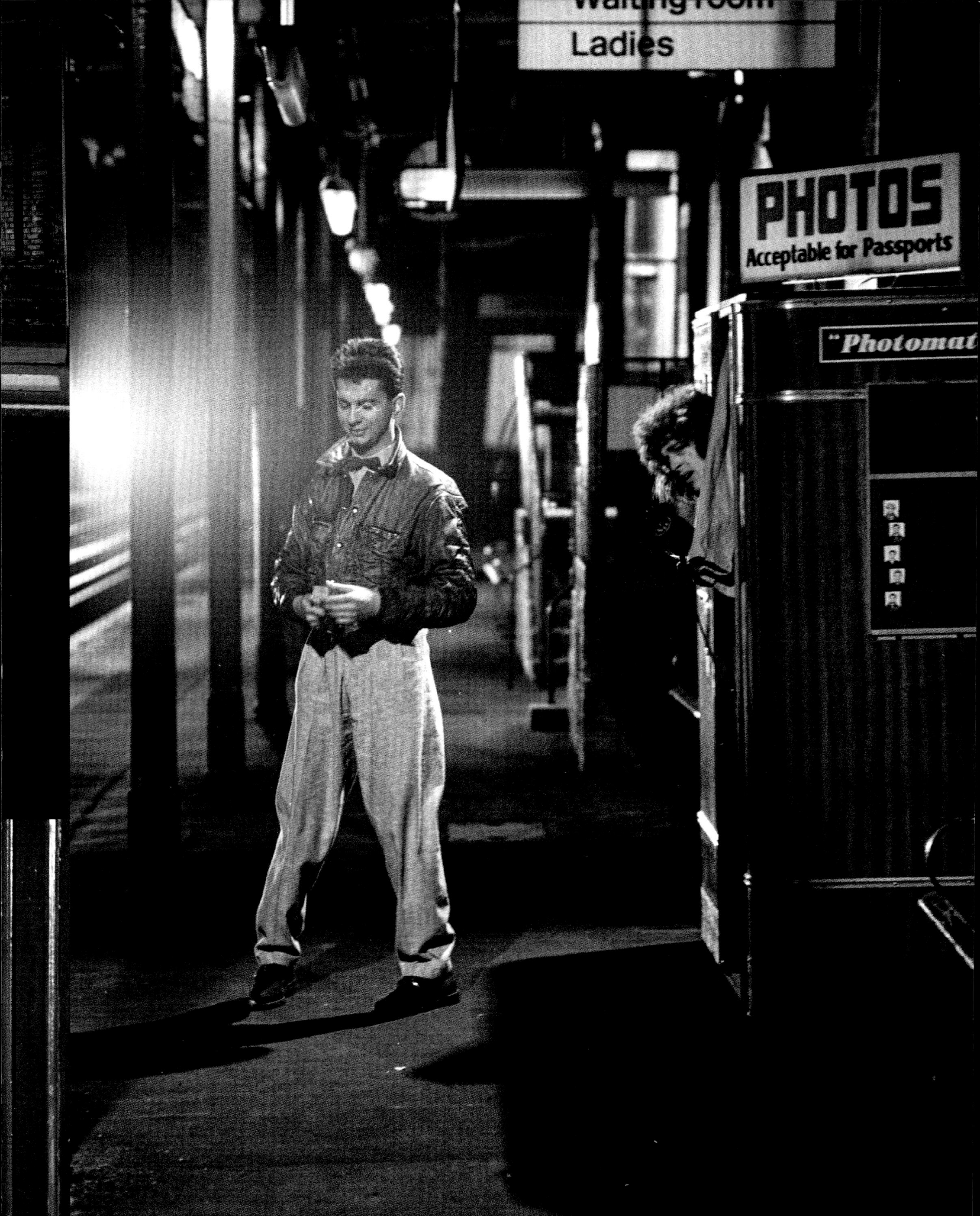
Ladies
PHOTOS
Acceptable for Passports
"Photomat

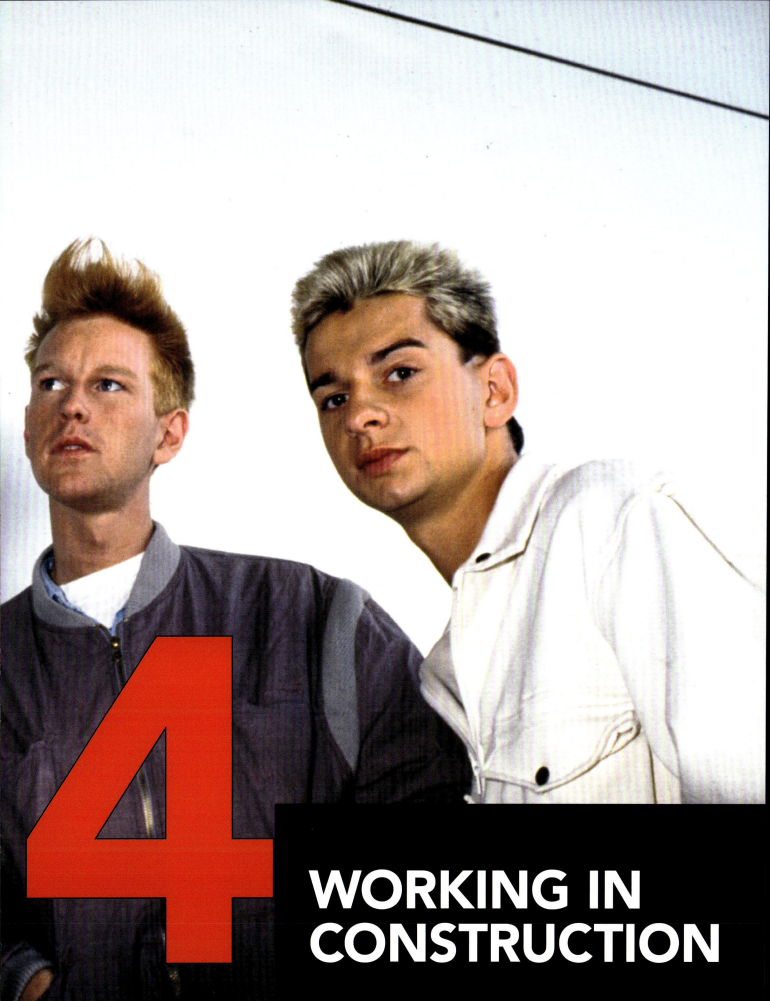

4

WORKING IN CONSTRUCTION

Daniel Miller had had a lot of good news to impart in the last few months. He had become a spectacular success in a role that he had fallen into entirely by accident.

It was only four years since Miller had founded Mute Records purely as a means to release his own records as The Normal, and maybe in-jokes such as the Silicon Teens. Now he was running a label with not one but two major chart-pop acts in Depeche Mode and Yazoo.

In pre-streaming 1982, when music fans swapped hard cash to own music on vinyl (and with the CD revolution right around the corner), this meant some serious money began to pour into Mute's coffers. Technophile that he was, Miller knew exactly how to spend it.

The Mute boss invested somewhere north of £10,000 (around £25k today) in a Synclavier II digital synthesizer. Made by the New England Digital Corporation of Vermont, this cutting-edge piece of equipment had just helped Quincy Jones to produce Michael Jackson's *Thriller*, now well on its way to becoming the best-selling album of all time.

The Synclavier II's crucial feature was its inbuilt polyphonic digital sampling system, which enabled users to make short recordings of real-world "found noises" (i.e. anything at all) and then manipulate them within music. This synth was to revolutionize the sound and feel of music—but initially, Depeche Mode found it a right palaver.

The band first encountered this game-changing technology before Christmas 1982, when they went back into Blackwing Studio—with Wilder, this time— at the request of Daniel Miller, to record a new single to keep the momentum of *A Broken Frame* going.

Martin Gore had come up with a slight, "See You"- like pop nugget, "Get the Balance Right!," which the band and Miller attempted to produce through the Synclavier. This was to prove a Herculean and hugely frustrating task. It was not love at first sight.

"The Synclavier was a state-of-the-art sampler/ synthesizer that sounded great," Alan Wilder was later to recall, semi-fondly, on his personal website, *recoil.co.uk*.

"It was an overpriced beast that took four grown men to assemble because of all its additional boxes, and it was a bit of a bastard to use. It was so expensive

PREVIOUS PAGE Depeche Mode, 1983

Mute Records' two chart-top stars: Depeche Mode, channeling Wham!, (**LEFT**) and Yazoo (**ABOVE**)

"It was an overpriced beast that took four grown men to assemble."

WILDER

that nobody could afford one, apart from one or two top producers."

It didn't help that Depeche weren't totally convinced of the merits of "Get the Balance Right!," but Miller was determined they should rush a single out and it was all they had. For days they battled the fearful Synclavier, recording version after version as they strove to, well, get the balances right.

Or, rather, Miller did: "Daniel's operating the Synclavier for us at the moment," the endearingly ingenuous Gore was to tell *Record Mirror*.

"Maybe in a year we'll be able to take over. The manual's very thick and it'd take us ages to work out how to use the thing . . . he just puts our ideas on it for us."

The torturous gestation of "Get the Balance Right!" was to turn the band against it: years later, Gore identified it as "our least favorite single. It was hell to record. I hate it, and I wrote it." Yet when it appeared, in January 1983, it was clear the dreaded Synclavier had given Depeche's sound a whole new depth and resonance.

Remarkably, it was also to prick up ears on the then-nascent Detroit techno scene. Despite not even being released in the US, "Get the Balance Right!" got played to death in the city's underground dance clubs, with Kevin Saunderson of Inner City famously going on to describe it as "the first house record." Depeche were to remain blissfully ignorant of this unlikely acclaim for many years to come.

The single charted at a respectable-but-not-great No. 13 in the UK and Depeche Mode set off on tour again. A one-off date in Frankfurt in February was scheduled to coincide with the Musikmesse musical instruments trade fair purely so they could check out the latest kit.

March found them back in the US, although the fact they had yet to make a commercial breakthrough in the States meant they were still playing fairly compact venues. It was the band's first trip to Asia the following month that made a bigger impression on them.

After playing two dates in Tokyo at the start of April, Depeche Mode were mobbed by five hundred fans at Kai Tak airport in Hong Kong. It was an experience they found unsettling—but not unpleasant.

"We wandered out into the airport pushing our bags on trollies when suddenly we were surrounded by hundreds of people who had come to meet us," they recounted in a tour program. "It was very frightening, but also very flattering. They had to call the police . . ."

Depeche then flew on to Thailand to play two shows at the Napalai Convention Hall in Bangkok. It was by far the most exotic destination the still-unworldly boys from Basildon had ever seen, and some of the scenes in the Thai capital shocked them.

Dave Gahan was appalled by the child beggars and open pedophilic exploitation he saw in Bangkok, while Martin Gore was horrified by the contrast between the wealthy Western businessmen in their luxurious hotels and the poverty-stricken young prostitutes outside offering up their bodies for a handful of baht.

Depeche Mode had never been a remotely socially conscious band—"We don't have political views, I don't think," Gahan had informed *Sounds*—but the Third World degradation in Bangkok made a lasting impression on Gore. It would also impact on their next album, which Gore began writing as soon as he was back in Britain.

"He wrote pretty much all the next album in a couple of weeks straight after those trips," Wilder was to report. "They seemed to come together pretty quickly and it was obvious that all these bizarre places such as Bangkok had opened up a few eyes in the band."

They had the songs and they had the cutting-edge equipment (even if they were a little fuzzy on how to work it). Yet going into their third album, Depeche were keen to rethink and reboot the way that they worked, in fresh surroundings and with new people around them.

> "We all wanted to discover new sound worlds, and give a sense of depth, scale and edge to the songs and music."
> JONES

John Foxx, owner of The Garden, in a garden

Having only ever recorded in Blackwing Studios, the band decided they wanted a change. Agreeing with them, Daniel Miller put in a call to one of the true pioneers of British electropop—John Foxx.

Foxx had left Ultravox in 1979 to record a solo album, *Metamatic*, whose austere, dystopian electro-futurism was both before its time and a major influence on, among others, a tyro Gary Numan. Foxx had used the money he had made from his follow-up, 1981's *The Garden*, to set up a recording studio of the same name.

Miller booked Depeche Mode into the Garden and Foxx suggested they make use of his in-house studio engineer, Gareth Jones, who had worked with him on *Metamatic*. Miller arranged for the band and the engineer to have an exploratory first meeting at Mute.

An attitudinal hippy-punk who lived in a squat in Brixton and was steeped in experimental electronica, Jones was skeptical about working with a band he regarded as featherweight fops churning out chart-friendly tinny ditties. However, as he talked to Depeche at Mute he was won round by their enthusiasm.

"It turned out that we had compatible approaches to the studio," he said in *Stripped*. "We all wanted to discover new sound worlds, and give a sense of depth, scale and edge to the songs and music."

Jones was also excited by the prospect of getting to grips with the Synclavier, which was duly installed in the Garden at the start of the sessions. Both he and the band were keen to collect found noises from real life to incorporate into the album, which by now had the working title of *Construction Time Again*.

They were in a good place to do so. Foxx's studio was in Shoreditch, east London. Nowadays a gentrified Mecca for artists and hipsters, in 1983 it was still largely a desert of abandoned factories, rundown wasteland, and building sites.

Going into making the album, Jones was enamored of a band that Martin Gore would also come to admire: Berlin-based, German post-punk noise

conceptualists Einstürzende Neubauten (a name that translates literally as "Collapsing New Buildings").

Neubauten's studio and stage instrumentation largely consisted of drills, pile drivers, and sledgehammers, with which they would beat heaps of corroding scrap metal. Industrial-music pioneers, they strove to capture the noise of manufacturing industry and society in decay: buildings collapsing around them.

Depeche Mode were always too beholden to tunes, melodies, and harmonies to become full-on avant-noise metal-bashers. However, excited by this philosophy and the potential of the Synclavier, they set out on a series of missions outside of the Shoreditch studio to gather interesting sounds and sonic textures.

The band and their producer and engineer spent hours roaming the streets throwing bricks at walls, smacking fences with pieces of wood or hitting lumps of corrugated iron and recording the results on a Sony Walkman. They felt like urban archaeologists, or post-industrial musical magpies.

"With Gareth Jones and Daniel Miller, it was like a pioneering expedition," Wilder was to tell *Sound on Sound* in 1998. "All of us would go off to derelict areas armed with a hammer and tape recorders."

"It was a revelation to us," Gore admitted to BBC television documentary *Synth Britannia* in 2009. "We were going out, smashing pieces of metal with sledgehammers, raiding the kitchen drawer for utensils to make percussion sounds. Anything we could get our hands on!

"There was one sample where we were hitting a piece of corrugated iron that was along the side of a building site, and the sample went, '*Krrraaang . . . oi!*' And the 'Oi!' was the site foreman!"

Back in the Garden, the band's technical gurus, Miller and Jones, fed these noises into the Synclavier, which was still demonstrating its capacity to be, as Wilder was to memorably describe it, "a bit of a bastard." Even the tech-wizard Jones found it frustrating: "We all had a love/hate relationship with the Synclavier," he admitted.

ABOVE Einstürzende Neubauten's Blixa Bargeld

RIGHT Pop stars, or post-industrial musical magpies?

Yet amalgamating these industrial noises into the mix would have been mere gimmickry if the songs were not there to support them. Luckily for Depeche Mode, Martin Gore had taken his songwriting game up a notch since the directionless sprawl of *A Broken Frame*.

The songs that Gore was bringing into the Garden for *Construction Time Again* sounded rich, poignant, and coherent. No longer fluffy and frivolous, there was newfound depth and determination among their lithe electro-grooves. There was also one standout track which appeared to tower over the others.

"We were going out, smashing pieces of metal with sledgehammers, raiding the kitchen drawer for utensils."

GORE

Inspired by the scenes of misery and economic inequality that Gore had witnessed in Bangkok, "Everything Counts" was a clumsy but sincere condemnation of the iniquities of capitalism. Its chorus was scarcely sophisticated, but it cut to the chase: "*The grabbing hands grab all they can/All for themselves, after all . . .*"

A haunting, tender melody based on a sample of a shawm (a Chinese oboe) expressed the vulnerability of the poor souls crushed by the wheels of industry, and by the business leaders chasing dollars: "*It's a competitive world/Everything counts in large amounts.*"

"It's about things getting out of hand," explained Gore in interview, with his trademark simplicity, "business getting to the point where individuals don't count, and you'll tread on anybody."

Elsewhere on the album, opener "Love, In Itself" was a querulous, knotted examination of the nature of infatuation. Delivered over a gorgeous, featherlike synth doodle, Dave Gahan's imposing dark-brown growl concluded that Cupid's arrow has its limitations: "*Love's not enough—in itself.*"

Written by Alan Wilder, "The Landscape is Changing" was an engaging electro-reverie on the theme of environmental destruction, while the oblique "Two Minute Warning" mused on nuclear oblivion. Both were worthy but likable, although Wilder never became a regular Depeche songwriter: as he later admitted on *recoil.co.uk*, it simply didn't come naturally to him.

The oddest song on *Construction Time Again* was "Pipeline," whose backing track was composed almost entirely of samples of the band's Neubauten-inspired

metal-bashing adventures around Shoreditch.

"Even the vocals [on that song] were recorded on location," Daniel Miller explained in *Depeche Mode: A Biography*. "We took the backing track out by the railway line in Shoreditch and Martin sang on location in an arch. You can hear the trains in the background, and all sorts of stuff."

As well as the heightened quality of the songs on *Construction Time Again*, the album also *sounded* so much richer and deeper, thanks to the cantankerous Synclavier. The dogged Gareth Jones had patently succeeded in his aim of giving "a sense of depth, scale and edge to the songs and music."

When it came time to mix the album, the Garden's 24-track studio was deemed not up to the task and so the band cast around for an alternative. The decision

they took was to change the mind-sets and lifestyles of the band—radically, for one of their number.

Gareth Jones visited Berlin to check out a local band and met up with Daniel Miller, who was there recording with new Mute signing Nick Cave and his soon-to-be-ex-band, The Birthday Party. Miller liked the city and readily agreed with Jones's suggestion to mix *Construction Time Again* there.

In July, Depeche Mode thus decamped to West Berlin and the 64-track mix room at the Hansa Tonstudio. This glistening, atmospheric complex had, to say the least, an evocative history.

Standing in the shadow of the Berlin Wall, Hansa had been the studio where David Bowie cut his iconic triptych of late-1970s albums, *Low*, *"Heroes,"* and *Lodger*, as well as overseeing and producing Iggy Pop's *The Idiot* and *Lust for Life*. From the studio control room, the group could see through the Iron Curtain into East Germany.

ABOVE Dave Gahan, backstage in Munich

LEFT Dave Gahan in Germany

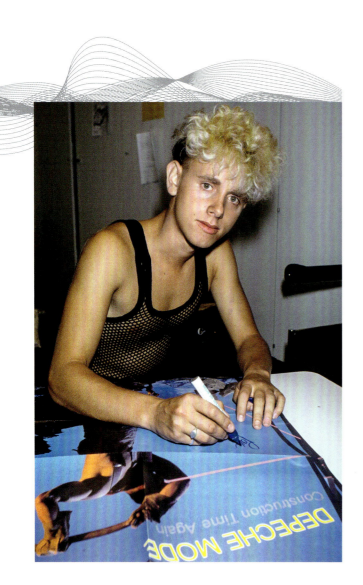

Martin Gore fell deeper in love with Berlin than anybody. A shy and naturally repressed soul, his inner timidity until then had been amplified by being in a long-term relationship with his childhood sweetheart, Anne Swindell, who was a devout Christian.

"She really had me on the reins," he admitted to *Uncut*. "She was ridiculous—*anything* was perverted! If I watched something on TV, and there was somebody naked, I was a pervert."

Gore had broken off his engagement to Swindell shortly before the mixing trip to Berlin and, newly enfranchised, threw himself into the edgy and sexual nightlife of the city. He also gained a new girlfriend in Berlin, a local named Christina Friedrich. "I suddenly discovered all this freedom," he admitted. "It was a big turning point for me."

It was a work-hard, play-hard time in Berlin, and every member of Depeche Mode took to the city. The mixing sessions went well, with running studio jokes including Andy Fletcher making an impromptu "solo album" called *Toast Hawaii*, named after his favorite meal in the studio canteen: cheese, ham and pineapple on toast.

There was even frivolous talk of Daniel Miller releasing this album on Mute. Thankfully, common sense prevailed: "It was pretty awful!" Fletcher admitted in 2001. "There's only one cassette copy I haven't seen for years . . . hopefully, it will never resurrect itself."

In advance of the release of *Construction Time Again*, "Everything Counts" came out as its lead single in July. A natural for daytime summer radio (despite its socialistic subject matter), it quickly became the band's best-selling hit to date, matching the No. 6 chart placing attained by "See You."

Meanwhile, Mute Records were readying the release of the album—a record whose cover was to excite higher than usual levels of comment.

For the sleeve image, photographer and designer Brian Griffin, who had also designed their two previous album covers, shot a shirtless, muscular ex-Marine wielding a sledgehammer high up a mountain in the Swiss Alps. The image seemed to mirror Soviet-style socialist realist art.

Taken with the new, halting social awareness of tracks such as "Everything Counts," and their recent sojourn by the Berlin Wall, the picture had commentators wondering whether Depeche Mode had taken a political left-turn. One journalist was particularly enamored of this theory.

Depeche Mode had by now toured Europe, America, and the Far East, but often had seen little of the cities they had visited outside of the routine of tour bus, soundcheck, hotel, gig, tour bus. In so many ways, they had seen the world while never leaving Basildon.

To their unworldly, still-inexperienced eyes, the bohemian, anything-goes atmosphere of Berlin was a revelation.

"It was a place full of artists and people interested in alternative lifestyles, and it's a 24-hour city," Daniel Miller told Steve Malins. "It was a very sexual place. It had a sense of eroticism, adventure and excitement . . . people had excessive lifestyles there, staying up for four or five days, taking a lot of drugs."

Working at Hansa until the early hours and then heading to one of the city's many all-night clubs, Depeche Mode went more than a little native in Germany, partying harder than they ever did in the UK. "Everyone got the Berlin vibe and started wearing black leather, me included!" Gareth Jones was to confess.

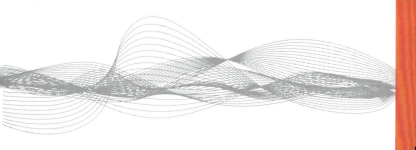

LEFT Martin Gore went native in Berlin

BELOW Who could ever call this man a pervert?

**"Depeche Mode have made
a bold and lovely pop record.
Simple as that."**

NME

Construction Time Again

TRACK LIST

SIDE ONE
Love, In Itself
More Than A Party
Pipeline
Everything Counts

SIDE TWO
Two Minute Warning
Shame
The Landscape Is Changing
Told You So
And Then . . .
Everything Counts (Reprise)

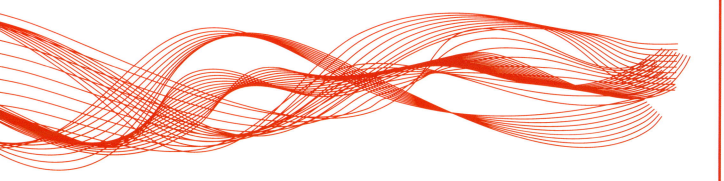

Recorded at The Garden, London, England

Produced by Daniel Miller & Depeche Mode

Personnel
Dave Gahan
Martin Gore
Andy Fletcher
Alan Wilder

Cover art
Brian Griffin: photography
Martyn Atkins: design

Released 22 Aug 1983

Label Mute STUMM 13

Highest chart position on release
UK 6, GER 7, FRA 16, NLD 32, NZ 44, SWE 12,
CAN 82, SWI 21

Socialist Workers Party member Chris Dean sang in a Marxist punk band named the Redskins and moonlighted as an *NME* writer under the pseudonym X. Moore. He interviewed Depeche and strove to establish their new crypto-communist credentials.

"When they finally come to bury their electro-wimp image, they do so not by firing off a couple of vitriolic anthems but with an album that argues patiently for organization," he wrote. "The theme of *Construction Time Again* is crystal-blatant."

Sadly for Dean/Moore, his reading of the record was so far off the mark that it left the band genuinely baffled. "X. Moore claims the album is virtually a rewrite of *The Communist Manifesto*," Fletcher was to marvel to *Melody Maker*. "I mean, that's just silly! The songs aren't so much political as songs of common sense."

"We're not trying to change anything," Gore concurred. "We're just trying to make people think a little bit . . . I don't think there's one of us

that's interested even slightly in politics." When *Construction Time Again* finally appeared on August 22, no other critics lauded it as a Marxist tract, but its wider sense of perspective and maturity was recognized. No longer discussing Depeche's "tinkly-bonk whimsy," *Smash Hits* noted that the band were now preoccupied with "the world (and all its problems)."

Rival chart-pop magazine *Number One* amusingly mislabeled Gore and Wilder's mildly political efforts "protest songs," but correctly lauded them for retaining "that distinctive ear for a pop melody." However, the best reading of the album came from Mat Snow, a rather more astute colleague of X. Moore.

Writing in *NME*, Snow said: "Dave Gahan's voice resounds with unsuspected strength and subtlety, and Martin Gore must now be regarded amongst our premier songwriters . . . Depeche Mode have made a bold and lovely pop record. Simple as that."

This critical approbation was echoed by the greater record-buying public. Seduced by "Everything Counts," they bought *Construction Time Again* in their droves, sending the album rocketing up the chart until it came to rest at No. 6.

It had entailed wrestling top-of-the-range equipment, hitting metal fences in Shoreditch, flirting with socialist realism, and frequenting eye-opening clubs in Berlin, but most importantly it had represented a musical and attitudinal breakthrough for Depeche Mode.

Now, they were about to go international—in more ways than one.

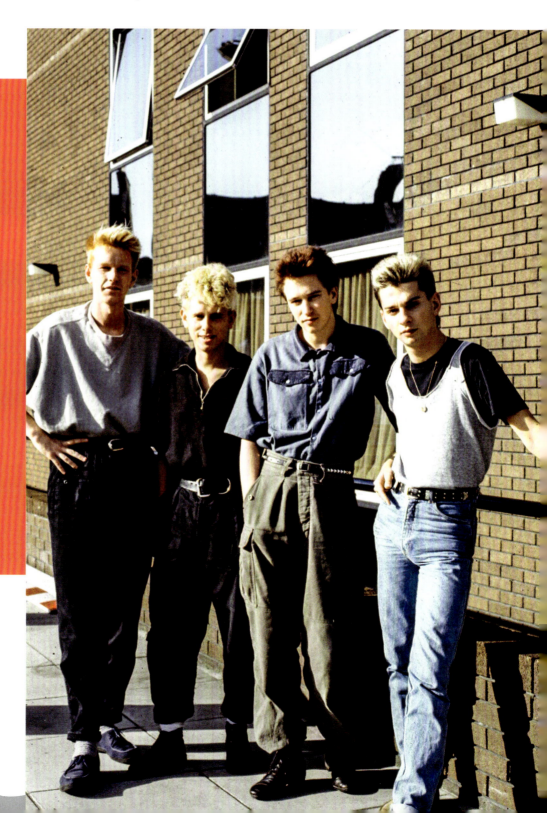

"Dave Gahan's voice resounds with unsuspected strength and subtlety, and Martin Gore must now be regarded amongst our premier songwriters."
NME

LEFT Depeche hit Hammersmith Odeon, 1983. Up next, 10cc and Shakin' Stevens

RIGHT "Is this photo shoot too glamorous?"

5
DEPECHE
ÜBER ALLES

Depeche Mode had all reveled in their stay in Berlin to mix *Construction Time Again*, but Martin Gore had gone one step further. He had fallen head over heels in love—both with his new girlfriend, Christina Friedrich, and with the city itself.

More than anybody else in their entourage, Gore had thrown himself into the city's demi-monde of all-night bars and parties, happening art scenes and galleries, and dance clubs that never shut. Usually Depeche's shyest and most self-censoring member, he had morphed into a full-on nocturnal party animal.

Just two years earlier, Gore had been processing standing orders in a NatWest bank every day and meekly toeing the line laid down by his devoutly Christian fiancée. Now, his social milieu included S&M sex clubs where cross-dressing was *de rigueur*.

By contrast, Dave Gahan had partied his way into juvenile delinquent centers a full five years earlier and was nowadays a largely reformed character in a steady relationship with a long-term girlfriend, Joanne Fox. He observed Gore's new hedonistic lifestyle with an almost paternal affection, as if to say: *It's always the quiet ones.*

"Martin's just being the way he always wanted to be," Gahan told one journalist. "He missed out on his teens, missed out on just going out, seeing different girls every night and getting drunk all the time.

"He's living that now. It's not a bad thing—everybody should go through that phase!"

When the *Construction Time Again* mixing party ended, Gore simply didn't want to go home and give up his new lifestyle—certainly not to live alone in grey London, or with his mother in Basildon. A few weeks after leaving Berlin, he rented an apartment with Christina in Charlottenburg, in the hedonistic heart of the city, and relocated to Germany full-time.

"I moved to Berlin because the 24-hour aspects of city life suits me," he freely confessed to *Number One*. "I'm happy to stay out all night. Is that decadent?"

Gore's decision was a personal lifestyle choice, but it also coincided with a sharp rise in Depeche's fortunes in his new chosen homeland. Having previously possessed only a small cult following there, the band were nonplussed to see *Construction Time Again* reach the Top 10 in Germany.

PREVIOUS PAGE Depeche Mode, German TV, 1984

LEFT The leather trouser years

RIGHT "It's always the quiet ones"

"Martin's just being the way he always wanted to be. He missed out on his teens, missed out on just going out."

GAHAN

"We never saw ourselves as having vaguely Germanic overtones to the music," Fletcher mused to *Smash Hits*. "If you've ever heard German pop music . . . I can't see the connection."

Although now domiciled in Berlin, Gore was spending a lot of time going back and forth to Britain: "I can be back in Basildon in two hours," he noted proudly to *Number One*. The band were about to do a lot more traveling as the *Construction Time Again* tour kicked into life in September.

Dave Gahan was becoming an increasingly confident and compelling front man, a writhing mass of agility and testosterone, but Depeche Mode's live show had always suffered from the fact that Gore, Fletcher, and Wilder were obliged to stand virtually static behind keyboards.

This time, they attempted to take the staging up a notch by placing the three keyboardists on podiums and incorporating an innovative light show based on three wooden towers dotted around the band. A long-time supporter, the *NME*'s Mat Snow, waxed lyrical at the tour's September opening night in Hitchin.

Describing Fletcher strolling onstage and turning on his keyboard, he rhapsodized: "By that casual push of a button, he sums up Depeche Mode's appeal: the technology of their music-making is instantly demythologised. You don't have to be a genius or rich or good-looking to stand a chance.

"Just like that other quartet of boys next door 20 years ago, Depeche Mode bridge the gap between performer and audience by showing the potential for magic in the most familiar, accessible things."

The Basildon Beatles? That was pushing it, but it was clear this was a significant tour for the band. Stressing the quantum leap they had taken on the album, the set list drew heavily on *Construction Time Again*, with early "Ultrapop" fluff such as "New Life" or "Just Can't Get Enough" chucked in as reluctant encores.

The UK dates climaxed with three nights at the Hammersmith Odeon in October, then after a short swing through Scandinavia and the Low Countries,

Depeche played no less than thirteen nights in Germany.

They had sold twice as many copies of *Construction Time Again* there as in Britain and many shows had to be upgraded to larger venues, including the ten-thousand-capacity Deutschlandhalle in Berlin. The tour ended with three sold-out pre-Christmas dates at the Musikhalle in Hamburg.

By contrast, the album had bombed in America, where radio stations had largely given it a wide berth, and the US and Canadian leg of the *Construction* tour was first postponed then cancelled completely. Speaking to *Smash Hits*, Dave Gahan was remarkably chipper about this apparent setback.

"We just had a meeting about America, and we decided not to worry about it," he declared, airily. "If we really wanted to be incredibly wealthy, we'd be over there trying to cash in on the British Invasion [the Human League, Duran Duran, and Culture Club were by then all doing well in the US], but *we don't see the point*."

"We never saw ourselves as having vaguely Germanic overtones to the music."

FLETCHER

LEFT Depeche Mode on TV . . .

BELOW . . . and on camera

It seemed that all roads now led to Deutschland for Depeche Mode, and when Daniel Miller came to choose a studio for them to record new material in January 1984, it was a no-brainer. The band would return to Hansa in Berlin.

Before that, they did a little pre-programming work in a rehearsal room in Dollis Hill, north London—where Martin Gore was to write a song that would change everything for the group.

"People Are People" sounded initially like an old-school, Vince Clarke-era Depeche nugget, all jaunty, summer-side-up melody and nimble synth lines. Lyrically, though, it was about as far from "New Life" as could be imagined.

With his trademark air of earnest curiosity, a puzzled Gore wondered aloud about the everyday existence of racism, homophobia, and the other negative traits that stopped people from just, like, getting along: "*I can't understand/What makes a man/Hate another man?*"

Gore drew on the experience of the physical and verbal abuse he had occasionally been subjected to on the streets of Basildon as a result of his defiantly different appearance. However, it was the plaintive chorus, delivered in the manner of a pre-teen badgering his parents for answers, that was to pass into lyrical infamy: "*People are people, so why should it be/You and I should get along so awfully?*"

The sentiment was heartfelt but the simplistic phrasing, clunky double-syllable rhyme, and prim "awfully" should have maybe alerted Depeche to the fact that it needed more work. For now, they were more delighted that it was a killer tune.

When the band and Daniel Miller arrived at Hansa they reunited with Gareth Jones, who had emulated Gore by falling for both Berlin and a local woman and

BELOW "Fletch, I've had this great idea for a lyric"
RIGHT Berlin boys, 1984

ABOVE "You'll catch your death of cold, Mart!"

LEFT Beneath the wall: in Hansa Studio, Berlin

moving to the city. They set about laying down the haunting, wide-eyed "People Are People."

There was the by-now-usual level of sonic innovation. Gahan sang his vocals through a PA into a huge hall at Hansa and the track featured heavily treated samples of both Gore swallowing and air passengers laughing and chatting on the flight over from London.

"There's very little playing going on in 'People Are People,'" Alan Wilder was to confirm to a technical journal, *International Musician and Recording World*. "Virtually everything was sampled into the Synclavier."

Yet studio trickery aside, the main point was that "People Are People" was a tremendous song, a shimmering synthesis of clattering beats, chiming keyboards, and an irresistible melody, with Gore adding his cherubic vocal to Gahan's stentorian drawl. It was an absolute shoo-in for a lead single.

With the song in the can, Depeche continued developing ideas for the record. Lyrically, this was the album on which Martin Gore's transformation from suburban Essex ingénue to keen observer of Berlin sex clubs became apparent.

Opening with a sample of Daniel Miller hissing into a mic to replicate the sound of a whip cracking, "Master and Servant" was clearly a song about S&M. "*You treat me like a dog*," crooned Gahan, gamely, "*Get me down on my knees*," before Gore's lyric went on to draw a rather trite analogy between sexual and societal domination.

Gore has always remained cleverly tight-lipped on whether he was a participant or a voyeur in Berlin's BDSM clubs, but there was no doubt he was still loosening up spectacularly.

"Sexual barriers are silly," he told *Number One* that year. "My girlfriend and I swap clothes, make-up, anything—so what?"

"If you listen very carefully [to 'Master and Servant']," advised Alan Wilder, "as well as the whip sounds, you can hear two Basildon girls singing, 'Treat me like a dog.'"

"Blasphemous Rumours" was equally taboo-bashing, this time of organized religion. Gore's lyrical tale of a teenage girl who survived a suicide attempt, found Jesus, and then died in a car crash built to the chorus suggestion that God had a "sick sense of humour."

Gore was to explain that the song was inspired by his early teenage churchgoing years in Basildon, where every week the vicar would read out a Prayer List of parishioners who were seriously ill or near to death, and then blithely thank the God who was about to snuff out their earthly life.

Showtime, 1984 and 1985

> # "When Martin first played me 'Blasphemous Rumours,' I was quite offended."
>
> **FLETCHER**

"It just seemed so strange to me," he told Steve Malins in *Depeche Mode: A Biography*. "So ridiculous, and so removed from real experiences."

"When Martin first played me 'Blasphemous Rumours,' I was quite offended," the lapsed churchgoer Fletcher was to admit. "I can see why people would dislike it. It certainly verges on the offensive."

The ballad "Somebody" found Gore crooning over piano declaring his undying love for his new amour, Christina. In an attempt to emphasize the sincerity and overwhelming passion of his feelings, he stripped off in the studio and recorded the song naked (away from the prying eyes of the rest of the band, which was probably best for all parties).

It was the track "Lie to Me" that was to lend the new album its name: *Some Great Reward*. Gore bemoaned the diminished role of truth in the world, with telling lies the norm in both personal relationships and wider life, before urging some unidentified protagonist to similarly deceive him: "*Make me think, that at the end of the day/Some great reward will be coming my way.*"

While self-admittedly not a natural songwriter, Alan Wilder was by now carving out a distinct role in the studio, playing a larger part in the music's arrangement and production. He would stay and work with Daniel Miller and Gareth Jones into the early hours as Gore, Gahan, and Fletcher vanished into the Berlin night to play.

The band took a break from the album in March to play a handful of final *Construction Time Again* tour dates in Eastern Europe, Italy, and Spain. As they came off the road, Mute released the "People Are People" single in the UK and Europe.

Gore's inadvertently comedic "*why should it be/get along so awfully*" rhyme inevitably gave rise to a few disbelieving sniggers: guest-reviewing for *Record Mirror*, Culture Club's Roy Hay admitted, "I really laughed the first time it came on."

No matter. "People Are People" was blatantly a magnificently classy earworm, a slick and superior slice of radio-friendly pop. Aided (or handicapped?) by an odd video of the band stalking around HMS *Belfast*, it became their highest-charting UK single, peaking at No. 4.

Germany was to better this. Despite their rapidly rising profile in the country, Depeche Mode had never had a Top 10 single there, their best effort to date having been "Everything Counts," which reached No. 23. This was about to change spectacularly.

Powered by being adopted by West German TV as a theme tune to their coverage of the 1984 Olympics in Los Angeles (possibly as a barbed comment on East Germany joining the Soviet Union-led boycott of the games), "People Are People" went to No. 1 for three weeks in West Germany—the band's first chart-topper anywhere in the world.

Indeed, so spectacular was Depeche Mode's sudden rise to fame in Germany that they were invited to play by far their biggest show to date: a one-off support date for Elton John at the forty-thousand-capacity Südweststadion in Ludwigshafen at the start of June.

Nerves were understandably jangling in the Mode camp, but Elton, well known for closely following new music and emergent artists, made a point of seeking out Martin Gore before their set to tell him how much he liked his songwriting and the band's music.

In stark contrast to the band hanging out with superstars in Germany, "People Are People" picked up very little airplay in America, where some FM radio stations remained suspicious of certain strains of British synth-pop. Like every previous Depeche single, it failed to chart, flopping ignominiously.

For now, anyway.

Having laid down the basis of *Some Great Reward* in Germany, the band came off the road and reconvened in Music Works Studio in north London to continue work on the album. The studio's location, near the busy Holloway Road, allowed them to continue foraging the streets for objects to bash.

"There were all these builders in next door to Music Works," Martin Gore was to admit. "We'd have the track running with us hitting skips and concrete, they'd be next door tearing a wall down, and we couldn't tell which one was which!"

On *The Tube* again, March 1984

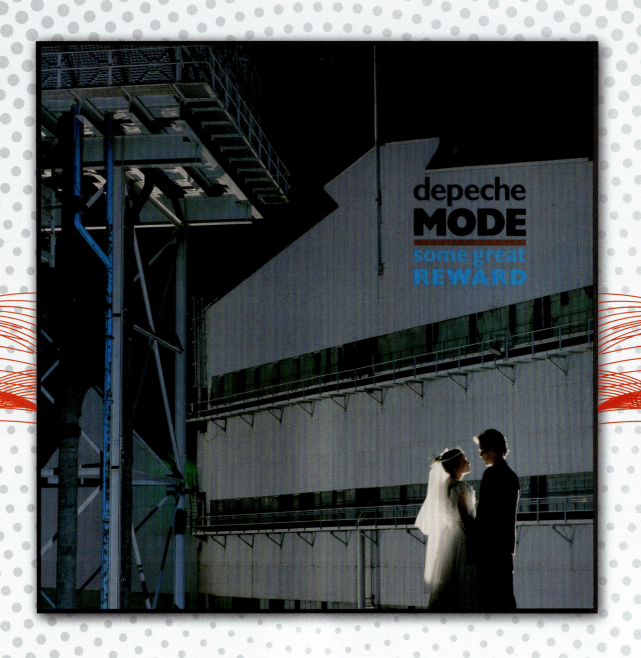

"Depeche have the right
balance and necessary gauche
[sic] to pull it off."

SOUNDS

Some Great Reward

TRACK LIST

SIDE ONE
Something to Do
Lie to Me
People Are People
It Doesn't Matter
Stories of Old

SIDE TWO
Somebody
Master and Servant
If You Want
Blasphemous Rumours

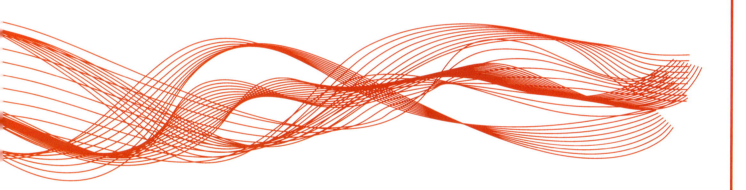

Recorded at Music Works, London, England & Hansa Tonstudio, Berlin, Germany

Produced by Daniel Miller, Gareth Jones & Depeche Mode

Personnel
Dave Gahan
Martin Gore
Andy Fletcher
Alan Wilder

Cover art
Brian Griffin: photography
Martyn Atkins: design

Released 24 Sept 1984

Label Mute STUMM 19

Highest chart position on release
UK 5, GER 3, FRA 10, NLD 34, NZ 44, SWE 7, CAN 34, SWI 5, US 54

Gore and Fletcher also paid a morning visit to Hamleys toy store in central London, returning to the studio with armfuls of children's pianos, xylophones, and marimbas. These toys, heavily treated and unrecognizable, popped up throughout the album.

Depeche Mode's bondage-lauding "Master and Servant" had come out as a single—going Top 10 in the UK and hitting a remarkable No. 2 in West Germany—when the band returned to Hansa to mix *Some Great Reward* in August.

This was to prove a painstaking process that Fletcher, Gahan, and Gore soon tired of. The trio went their separate ways on summer holidays with their partners, leaving Miller, Jones, and the keen-to-be-involved Wilder to complete the mixing process.

As the band members returned from the beach, *Some Great Reward* was released at the end of September. In the UK, the album received the traditional critical reception of grudging admiration of Depeche's songcraft, mixed with patronizing reminders of the group's supposed tackiness.

"It used to be OK to slag this bunch off," commented *Melody Maker*, "but [the album] demands you now sit up and take notice of what is happening here, right under your nose."

Number One declared that Depeche Mode were "sadly underrated" and praised them for "progressing a million miles from their boppy origins" but nevertheless found (understandable) fault with the album: "Martin Gore's lyrics haven't kept up. Over a whole LP, their gaucheness is a major distraction from the record's musical merits."

This idea was echoed by *Sounds*, which also dished out praise with one hand and took it back with the other: "OK, the lyrics look trite, often naïve and frequently clichéd . . . yet Depeche have the right balance and necessary gauche [sic] to pull it off."

As usual, the increasingly devoted Depeche Mode disciples cared little for what the critics thought. *Some Great Reward* sold more than eighty thousand copies in its first two weeks of UK release, hitting a new chart high point of No. 5. In West Germany, it was to reach No. 3.

Even more significantly, the record was to score the band's first real chart action in America. Its highest placing, No. 54, may have been unspectacular, but *Some Great Reward* was doggedly to spend forty-two weeks on the chart. Underground word of mouth was growing.

Three days after the album appeared in the UK, the band took off on a three-month British and European tour, with North American and Japanese dates penciled in for the following year. Their on-the-road jaunts were growing in size and, this time, in spectacle.

An ambitious stage set saw the band on ramps and risers amongst quasi-industrial strip lights, sheets of metal, and neon tubes as sporadic projections of stained-glass windows flashed behind them. Yet for many audience members, the most jaw-dropping attraction was standing behind the middle of the three keyboards.

Shaped by swinging Berlin, Martin Gore's stage (and offstage) image now incorporated eyeliner, lipstick, black nail varnish, leather straps worn tight across a bare chest, and leather miniskirts. Was this a return to glam-rock androgyny, or full-on transvestism?

Gore's adopted look would raise eyebrows anywhere in the world, not just down Basildon High Street. While largely supportive of his fashion whims, his less splashy bandmates occasionally suggested that he might like to, you know, *tone it down* a bit.

"I was never comfortable with Martin dressing up in girls' clothing," Alan Wilder was later to admit. "The rest of the group often used to comment to try to dissuade him. But I think the more we might do that, the more belligerent he'd become about it, so he had his mind made up."

In the same *Uncut* interview, Gore was to confess that while he was fiercely defensive of his extreme

"Martin, it's just . . . could you maybe? . . . Oh, it doesn't matter"

S&M fashion phase (which lasted about two years) at the time, in later life he was less sure what it was all about.

"I honestly don't know what was going through my head while I was doing that," he admitted, with beguiling candor. "There was some kind of sexuality to it that I liked and enjoyed but I look back now and see a lot of the pictures, and I'm embarrassed."

As the *Some Great Reward* tour wended its way across Britain, Mute put out "Blasphemous Rumours" in October as the album's third single. Future Pet Shop Boys star Neil Tennant, then *Smash Hits* assistant editor, was reliably acerbic: "A routine slab of gloom in which God is given a severe ticking off," he noted, tartly.

With radio stations loath to play it, suspecting sacrilegious content, the contentious single stalled in the lower reaches of the Top 20 in the UK (although, interestingly, it leapt to No. 8 in Catholic Church-dominated Ireland).

"A routine slab of gloom in which God is given a severe ticking off."
TENNANT

Dave Gahan, Canada, 1985 on the *Some Great Reward* tour

"It's not a bad thing to be religious," a sanguine Martin Gore told *Melody Maker*. "I think I'd be happier if I *did* believe." But the single's under-performance was no more than a minor irritant.

Suddenly it seemed as if, particularly outside Britain, Depeche Mode were inexorably on the rise. A pre-Christmas month of European shows saw them sell out a slew of indoor arenas in Germany as well as their first major gig in previously resistant France, at Paris's Palais Omnisports de Paris-Bercy.

And even further afield, across the Atlantic, something was brewing.

Having died the death on its initial summer 1984 release, "People Are People" had enjoyed a second wind in the US, powered in part by the support of hip Los Angeles radio station KROQ. A Sire compilation album, also called *People Are People*, had increased awareness, and *Some Great Reward* had been climbing the *Billboard* chart for weeks.

Word began to filter back that ticket sales for Depeche Mode's first significant US tour, in March 1985, were looking deeply encouraging. It gave the band a confidence boost and a following wind as they returned to Hansa and Berlin at the start of that month to record a new single, "Shake the Disease."

Given the original working title of "Understanding," the first few lines suggested that Gore was revisiting his S&M lyrical fixation. "*I'm not going down on my knees, begging you to adore me . . .*" growled Gahan, who had recently taken singing lessons (not particularly enjoying them) from renowned vocal coach Tona de Brett.

Yet "Shake the Disease" was a gentle, brooding little number in which a tongue-tied but sincere lover pledged devotion to his girl. It was valiant rather than vintage Mode, a tad "Love, In Itself" redux, and was only a minor hit in the UK (the reliably fervent German fans were keener, taking it to No. 4).

Now it was time for America.

Martin Gore had unhappy memories of the band's pair of previous under-powered attempts to break the States: "We seemed to be defending ourselves wherever we went, and we almost gave up on America." This visit was to be very different.

Thanks to "People Are People" and the evangelical support of KROQ, most of the sixteen dates, kicking off in Washington, D.C. on March 14, had sold out before their plane even touched down. Where previous US Depeche crowds had been too cool for school, now the audiences at venues like New York's prestigious Beacon Theatre were suddenly wildly into them.

Canadian shows in Montreal and Toronto were equally frenzied, and then the band returned to America to packed houses in Chicago and at the vast Bronco Bowl in Dallas. Los Angeles's historic Hollywood Palladium on Sunset Strip had sold out in fifteen minutes flat.

Californians in particular just could not get enough of Depeche Mode. A further sold-out SoCal show was riskily upgraded by the promoter to the fifteen-thousand-capacity Irvine Meadows Amphitheatre. This also sold out.

MTV was beginning to love them (despite the fact that their videos to date had been of questionable quality), and by the time Depeche filled the voluminous San Diego Sports Arena and Oakland Civic Auditorium, it was clear that everything had changed for a band *still* viewed in their homeland as provincial and parochial.

Having conquered Germany, Depeche Mode stood on the verge of the holy grail of all British artists and record labels (even ones as radical as Mute)—breaking America. This promised land was over the next few years to bring them vast fame and riches as it became their playground, their haven . . . and their hell.

Along the way, it would also come close to killing them.

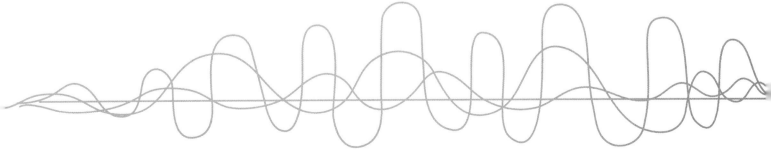

6

"GOOD EVENING, PASADENA!"

Having seen their fortunes rise in the US, Depeche Mode stayed on the road in the summer of 1985, playing a handful of dates in Japan then setting off on a mini-tour of European festivals. Three dates in France spoke of heightened interest in them, but the Euro dates had distinct highs and lows.

At their first Eastern European gig, on Martin Gore's twenty-fourth birthday, fans in Hungary's eight-thousand-capacity Volan Stadium serenaded him with "Happy Birthday." It was more fun than the Rock in Athens festival three days later, alongside Culture Club, the Cure, the Clash, and the Stranglers, where Boy George was bottled off as anarchists rioted. When Gahan went shopping the next day, he was punched in the face.

It had not escaped the shrewd Daniel Miller's notice that, quietly and unobtrusively, Depeche Mode had become a killer singles band. He decided to release a greatest hits album and, back in Britain, they went into fabled electropop producer Martin Rushent's Genetic Studios to make a new single to feature on it.

Ironically, this single to promote their singles proved a bit of a damp squib. The upbeat, Gore-penned "It's Called a Heart" was a jog on the spot. Insipid and lacking a memorable tune, it barely scraped into the Top 20. Wilder was years later to describe it as his "least favorite ever Depeche Mode single."

This disappointing performance was not repeated by the album it heralded. Released in October 1985, *The Singles 81–85* reached No. 6 in Britain, and reviewers finally caught up with fans' realization that Depeche Mode were a classy pop band.

"As the tracks rolled by . . . the truth became apparent," noted Stuart Maconie in *NME*. "It was only when you heard their career in this way, compressed into nuggets of excellence and strung together like pearls, that the truth hit you. Depeche Mode are one of the great exponents of the pop single on the planet."

PREVIOUS PAGE Depeche Mode, 1986
LEFT Who knew? A killer singles band
BELOW At Kiyomizu temple in Kyoto, Japan, 1985

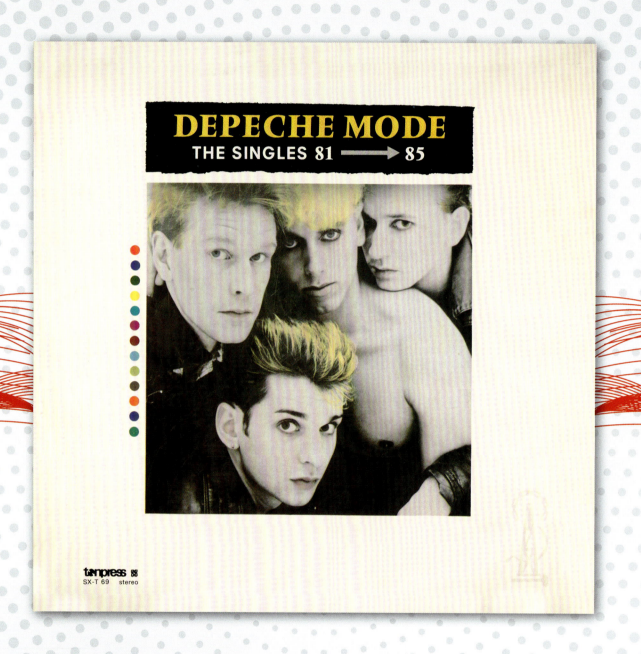

"Depeche Mode are one of the great exponents of the pop single on the planet."

STUART MACONIE, *NME*

The Singles 81–85

TRACK LIST

Dreaming of Me
New Life
Just Can't Get Enough
See You
Leave in Silence
Get the Balance Right
Everything Counts

Love in Itself
People Are People
Master and Servant
Blasphemous Rumours
Shake the Disease
It's Called A Heart

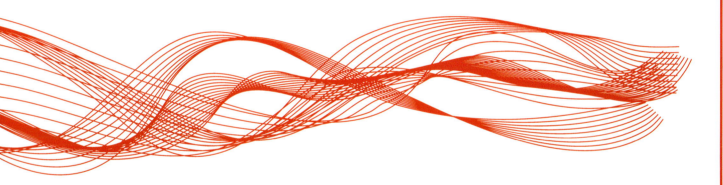

Recorded at Blackwing Studios, The Garden, Music Works, London; Genetic Studios, Streatley, England; Hansa Tonstudio, Berlin, Germany

Produced by Daniel Miller, Gareth Jones & Depeche Mode

Personnel
Dave Gahan
Martin Gore
Andy Fletcher
Alan Wilder
Vince Clarke

Cover art
Martyn Atkins

Released 14 Oct 1985

Label Mute MUTEL 1

Highest chart position on release
UK 6, GER 9, FRA 7, SWE 18, SWI 14

Amusingly, the inner sleeve of the record reprinted press reviews of each of the singles—both positive and negative. Neil Tennant's arch dismissal of "Blasphemous Rumours" made the cut. "It was just for a laugh," Gore shrugged to one journalist, "and to say *we don't really care*."

Striking while the iron was heating, Sire also released a second US Mode compilation album, shoehorning their most recent singles and B-sides onto a record called *Catching Up with Depeche Mode*. The goal appeared to be consolidation, on both sides of the Atlantic.

Yet the band were now going through a distinctly turbulent patch. They were being pulled in different directions. While Gahan had recently married Jo Fox and bought a house in suburban Essex, Gore was still cross-dressing and all-night partying in Berlin. That was OK: more pressing were their professional differences.

Exhausted from months of touring, Depeche had decided to take a couple of months off before beginning work on their next album. When they met up in west London that autumn, tensions showed as confusion reigned.

"If we were ever going to split up the band it was at the end of 1985," Dave Gahan was to confess to *Melody Maker*, five years later. "We were really in a state of turmoil. Constant arguing. Very intense.

"We weren't really sure where to go after *Some Great Reward* so we decided to slow things down. But it left us with too much time on our hands, and we spent most of the time arguing. It seems incredible we came out of that period with the band and our sanity intact."

This new mood of intra-band conflict was too much for the hypersensitive Gore who went into hiding for a week or so, staying with a German exchange-trip friend from school on his farm in Schleswig-Holstein. "I freaked out," he later confessed. "I had to go away for a few days."

RIGHT Back in harness: Martin Gore
BELOW Months of touring took their toll

Depeche Mode reconvened at Westside Studios in west London to discover Daniel Miller had devised a master plan for the making of their new album. He decreed that they should record it in one four-month unbroken session—with no days off.

"I was very influenced by [German film director] Werner Herzog," he told Steve Malins in *Depeche Mode: A Biography*. "They were all historical films, and people really *lived* the films, and it was a very intense way of working."

With Gore also intent on making "a lot heavier, harder and darker" album than *Some Great Reward*, the scene was set for what can safely be called a "difficult" recording process. The atmosphere making the album that was to become *Black Celebration* reflected at least half of the record's title.

The songs that Gore was taking into the studio were more ambient and less beholden to melodies and conventional song structures. They were also notably darker in tone, despite inevitably being undermined by Gore's usual unintentionally comedic lyrics: "Death is everywhere," noted the opening line of "Fly on the Windscreen." "There are flies on the windscreen . . . *for a start*."

Black Celebration was clearly not going to be a pop album and Gore was keen to color it in the darkest hues. His sole instruction to the production team of Miller and Gareth Jones was that there should be lots of reverb. "The band had decided that reverb = atmosphere," Jones later said. "And we went for it, big time."

Having begun work in London, the band soon switched back to Berlin and Hansa. The issues that were to plague the album went with them. The primary problem was bony elbows behind the mixing desk.

On all four previous Depeche albums, Daniel Miller had played the shaping role in the studio. His ideas largely went unchallenged. By now, however, Alan Wilder had grown considerably more skilled on the console and was keen to have more influence on proceedings.

With Gareth Jones also again co-producing, *Black Celebration* was in danger of becoming a musical broth spoiled by too many studio cooks. It could get very crowded behind that studio glass.

"The lines of our roles grew a lot more blurred during the making of the album," Miller was to reflect in *Depeche Mode: A Biography*. "Gareth was more

involved in production. We were together every day and we were starting to step on each other's toes.

"Alan was becoming very adept in that studio-bod role which I'd filled before. That left my own position less defined but I still had a very strong point of view. I think that created a lot of tension."

As well as the push-me, pull-me behind the studio console, the band were simply working for too long without the release of a day off. Combined with the copious amounts of weed being smoked in Hansa, soon an air of edgy paranoia permeated the sessions.

With Miller, Jones, and Wilder still wrestling over the controls of the Synclavier, Depeche remained in thrall to the joys of sampling. If anything, they embraced it harder than ever: "We had this theory at the time that every sound must be different and you must never use the same sound twice," Fletcher was to say in Stripped.

The grueling sessions were not without their lighter moments. On Bonfire Night, the producers set up a string of microphones along the asphalt on the studio car park and fired rockets over them. "It was probably the most dangerous bit of sampling we've ever done!" said Miller.

"We were together every day and we were starting to step on each other's toes."

MILLER

PREVIOUS PAGE Live on stage at Ahoy in Rotterdam, 1986

LEFT "What? No days off?"

BELOW Dave Gahan escapes the studio tensions

"I do think the album's claustrophobic feel was probably down to the tension."

WILDER

RIGHT Filming the "Stripped" music video
BELOW On TV: chirpy doodles were out, dark atmospherics were in

Mostly, though, the atmosphere was torturous as the intentionally backbreaking production schedule took its toll. The air of insular intensity extended to the Hansa mixing sessions, with Miller, Jones, and Wilder spending days in a quest for perfection, micro-tweaking or scrapping mixes until the band had to step in to ask them to get a grip.

Black Celebration had endured a truly painful birth—but maybe it had all been worth it. "I do think the album's claustrophobic feel was probably down to the tension," mused Wilder later. "I think it did add a chemistry to the sound of the record, more than any others we have done. It's one of my favourite records we have ever made."

Black Celebration was heavy on mood pieces and darkly brooding atmospherics but not big on pop tunes. Its lead single, "Stripped," was a fantastic play-frame for Gahan's tremulous, velvet baritone, but "A Question of Lust" and "A Question of Time" were gloomy, ambient throbs, albeit highly seductive ones.

In many ways, *Black Celebration* was the first album made entirely in line with Gore's intuited vision of the band, with no chirpy "People Are People"-style pop doodles thrown in to leaven the mix. It was a mechanistic, thrumming whole rather than an amalgam of would-be hits and filler tracks. And it was all the better for it.

Gore's heightened control was illustrated by the fact that he sang no less than four tracks on the album: the gentle "A Question of Lust," "Sometimes," "It Doesn't Matter Two," and "World Full of Nothing." "We've noticed that my voice is more suited to the softer and slower songs than Dave's," he told *MT* magazine on the record's release.

As usual, UK critics greeted its appearance by stroking their chins and mildly patronizing the group. *NME*'s Sean O'Hagan felt that its mood was "dark but faintly ridiculous." In *Melody Maker*, regular Depeche tormenter Steve Sutherland found it "depressing" that the band had "only managed to trade in one set of clichés for another—white for black, bright for bitter, tunes for twisted chants."

Yet *Smash Hits*' perceptive Chris Heath had a rather better handle on the album.

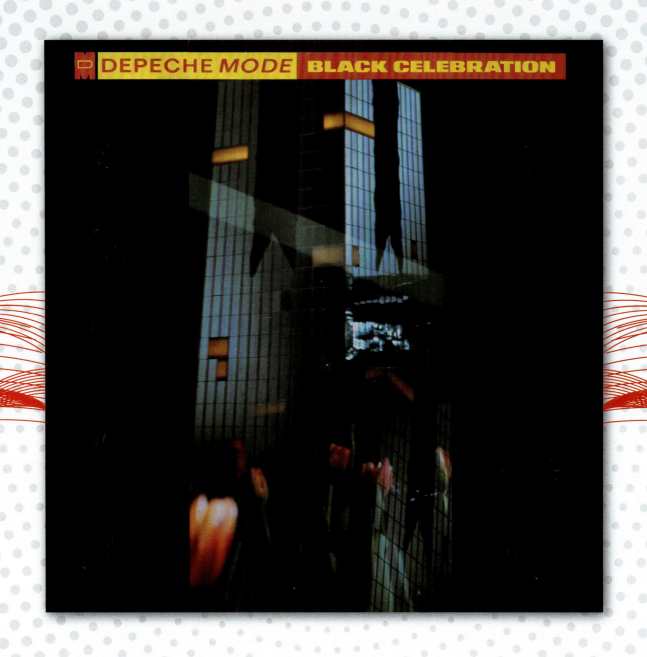

"*Black Celebration* doesn't only see
them go a bit weirder . . . it's also the
first time they haven't had to throw
in any second-rate stodge.
Their best album yet."

SMASH HITS

Black Celebration

TRACK LIST

SIDE ONE
Black Celebration
Fly on The Windscreen - Final
A Question of Lust
Sometimes
It Doesn't Matter Two

SIDE TWO
A Question of Time
Stripped
Here Is the House
World Full of Nothing
Dressed in Black
New Dress

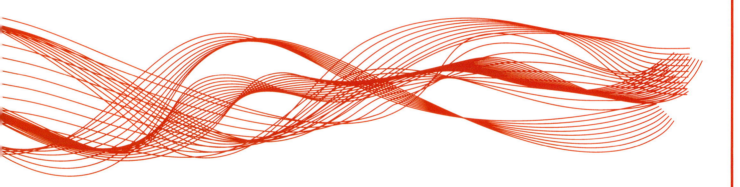

Recorded at Westside and Genetic, London, England & Hansa Tonstudio, Berlin, Germany

Produced by Daniel Miller, Gareth Jones & Depeche Mode

Personnel
Dave Gahan
Martin Gore
Andy Fletcher
Alan Wilder

Cover art
Brian Griffin: photography
Martyn Atkins: design

Released 17 Mar 1986

Label Mute STUMM 26

Highest chart position on release
UK 4, GER 2, FRA 11, NZ 34, SWE 5, CAN 47, SWI 1, US 90, ITA 9, AUS 69

"*Black Celebration* doesn't only see them go a bit weirder with lots of dark, mysterious percussive episodes (sung by Dave Gahan) snuggling up against sweet, fragile and rather sinister ballads (sung by Martin Gore)," he noted, "but it's also the first time they haven't had to throw in any second-rate stodge. Their best album yet."

Unlike all previous Depeche Mode albums, none of the singles from *Black Celebration* reached the Top 10, but this was not to prove any kind of setback. The album peaked at No. 4 in the UK, their best performance to date.

It is a classic hallmark of a cult band: albums that fly out of the shops even if singles stall on the launch pad. And the ensuing *Black Celebration* tour was to prove that Basildon's finest were rapidly becoming one of the biggest cult bands in the world.

As usual, the British dates went up a notch: two nights at the NEC in Birmingham, two at Wembley Arena. Germany was also reliably adulatory, necessitating two separate visits to the country to soak up the demands for their shows there.

It was America, though, that was to surprise Depeche Mode this time around. On the surface *Black Celebration* had underperformed in the US, peaking at a chart high of No. 90, nearly forty places lower than *Some Great Reward*. This was not reflected in live ticket sales.

Once announced, Depeche's American gigs sold out in a flash, with more and more nights having to be added. There were three at New York's nearly six-thousand-capacity Radio City Music Hall alone, while the tour was to climax with two sold-out open-air shows to sixteen thousand people each at the Irvine Meadows Amphitheatre in California.

For a band routinely mocked in their homeland, with the sum total of one US hit single to their name, it was a stunning achievement that left them pleased but perplexed. As Martin Gore was to note: "We were playing to more people than we were selling records to in the States. We could sell out everywhere we played."

The astute Wilder hit on a possible explanation for this rarefied new status. "It seemed we fitted in perfectly with what the all-American, white, middle-class kids seemed to be searching for," he surmised to Stephen Dalton of *Uncut* in 2001.

PREVIOUS PAGE On the "Stripped" video shoot

RIGHT Skimpy shorts and slip-on shoes in American stadia

"[We were] a band that was clean enough to crossover but subversive enough to push a few boundaries at the same time. I think we felt good about that and enjoyed sticking two fingers up to England with its provincial attitude."

The tour was visually spectacular, playing out on a set design based on Leni Riefenstahl's film of the infamous 1936 "Hitler Olympics" and lit up by spectacular illuminations. Offstage the band were drinking and partying hard, with Gore particularly prone to epic excess.

"Martin was always a big drinker," confirmed Wilder in *Depeche Mode: A Biography*. "When he's drunk he's the exact opposite to the shy person he is in everyday life. He says the most bizarre things . . . he's your best mate in the evening, but the next morning he's back to quiet Martin again."

As the band rounded off the tour with a final slew of European dates in August 1986, they released "A Question of Time" as the final single from *Black Celebration*. While this fact was unremarkable in itself, it was to trigger a sea change in the band's image.

Dodgy dress sense, self-consciousness, and a stream of inexperienced directors had meant that Depeche videos had largely been a string of car crashes to that point. Yet for "A Question of Time" Mute hired the none-more-arty Dutch *NME* photographer and fledgling video-maker Anton Corbijn.

Corbijn, who had already made videos for Echo & the Bunnymen and begun the Herculean task of overhauling U2's image, shot a typically classy and brooding monochrome vid that mixed live footage with a storyline that saw a biker find a baby in the desert and present him to the band.

"We shot it, and I didn't hear from them for nine months," Corbijn was to admit. "I thought they must have really hated it!" No—it was just another Depeche Mode communication failure. His art-house cinematography fitted Depeche Mode like a glove and a long, fertile, and productive relationship was to ensue.

As one figure entered Depeche's orbit, another left it. Planning the follow-up to *Black Celebration*, the band were keen to shake up their *modus operandi*—

that album's painful production process had felt a tad *fin de siècle*. After three albums, they decided to say goodbye to Gareth Jones.

Mindful of his studio clashes with Jones and Wilder, Daniel Miller also stepped away from the album's production to concentrate on developing Mute's roster. There was a neat irony in that the group then selling most records for the label in the UK, and enjoying the highest profile, was Vince Clarke's latest pop project, Erasure.

Despite Alan Wilder's increased studio suss, Depeche were therefore in the market for a co-producer for the album that was to become *Music for the Masses*. They settled on one Dave Bascombe, who had worked as a studio engineer for Peter Gabriel and Tears for Fears, including the latter's US No. 1 album, *Songs from the Big Chair*.

It was a time of quiet upheaval for the band members. Dave Gahan and his wife, Jo, were expecting their first child. Martin Gore had ended his love affair with Christina and with Berlin, and moved back to London. Now equipped with a home studio,

"A band that was clean enough to crossover but subversive enough to push a few boundaries."

GAHAN

LEFT Anton Corbijn reinvented Depeche's visual image
BELOW "Not Vince again!" The rise of Erasure

Alan Wilder had begun recording experimental electronica under the name Recoil—and Daniel Miller had begun releasing it.

This home studio was where Gore initially played Bascombe and the band his song demos for *Music for the Masses*. They then decamped to Paris, where the album was to be recorded at the Studio Guillaume Tell in a former cinema on the left bank of the Seine.

If it sounded a romantic setting, the reality was more prosaic. "We stayed in this place in the city that was christened 'Turd City' because everybody there had a dog," Wilder was to complain in *Stripped*. "There were turds all the way around it."

Hiring Bascombe was a major indication that Depeche were keen to rethink their way of doing things on the new album. Yet old habits die hard, so they spent their first few days in Paris walking around bashing things and recording the sounds. However, they did relax the synthesizer-only policy that dated from the Vince Clarke era.

Martin Gore played guitar—heavily treated and processed, naturally—on the album's opening, key track, "Never Let Me Down Again." This rich,

redolent, apparent musing on the joys of narcotic abandon was a sophisticated delight, even if you did wince at Gore's rhyming of "*safe as houses*" with "*wearing the trousers*."

"Never Let Me Down Again" was certainly a stronger, deeper offering than the album's lead single, "Strangelove," a relatively lightweight Gore piece. A mid-chart plodder in the UK, it nevertheless hit No. 2 in Germany and made a small mark in the clubs of the US.

With Bascombe arguably filling the role of a senior engineer rather than an agenda-shaping producer, the atmosphere in the studio was more relaxed than during the fraught *Black Celebration* sessions. Bascombe was to speak of a band obsession with getting "all the beats perfect" but the record that emerged sounded sleek, sultry, and assured.

The purring "The Things You Said" dug deep into the psyche to dissect fear, vulnerability, and relationships: "*You know my weaknesses/I've never tried to hide them.*" "Sacred" found Gahan crooning the flawed words of a religious missionary. "Behind the Wheel," a future single, was both a road song and a plea to be dominated. This was strong, powerful material.

"We had become aware of highs and lows," Dave Gahan was later to enthuse to the press. "We were conscious of building up atmospheres, heightening the songs to an absolutely massive feeling and then bringing them down again. We had discovered dynamics. It was our first truly *arranged* album."

When work in the City of Light and Dog Turds was done, Daniel Miller joined the band at Puk Studios, in north Denmark, to help to mix the album. He was responsible for remixing the pert and perky single "Strangelove" into a far heftier, slower beast for the album.

Music for the Masses was released on September 28, 1987. And what did the strange, apparently self-deprecating title mean? "It's a joke," reckoned Gore. "I think our music never crosses over to the general public. It's only the fans who buy our stuff."

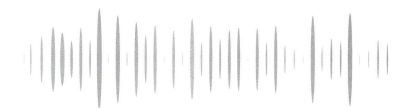

"We were conscious of building up atmospheres . . . we had discovered dynamics. It was our first truly *arranged* album."

GAHAN

LEFT Onstage at the RDS Arena, Dublin, April 1986

BELOW Table football in the studio: "Keep it tight at the back, Fletch!"

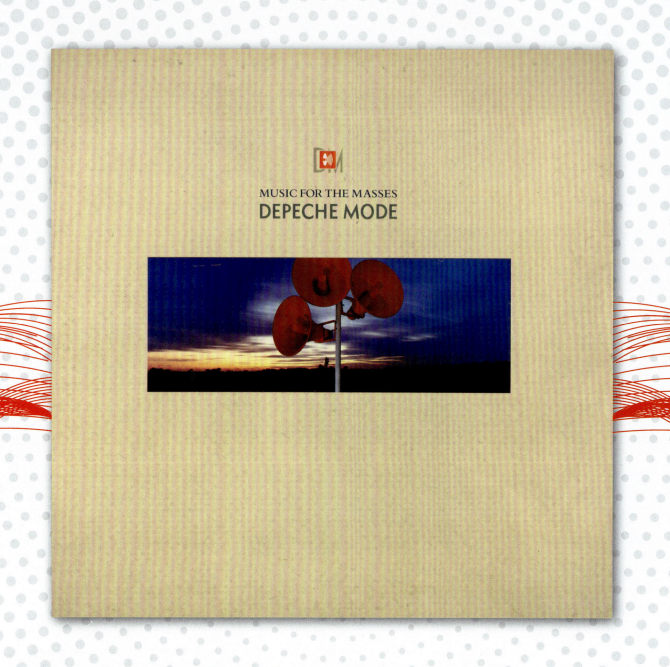

"Depeche Mode are
unashamed pop entertainers."
NME

Music for the Masses

TRACK LIST

SIDE ONE
Never Let Me Down Again
The Things You Said
Strangelove
Sacred
Little 15

SIDE TWO
Behind the Wheel
I Want You Now
To Have and To Hold
Nothing
Pimpf / Interlude #1" (hidden track)

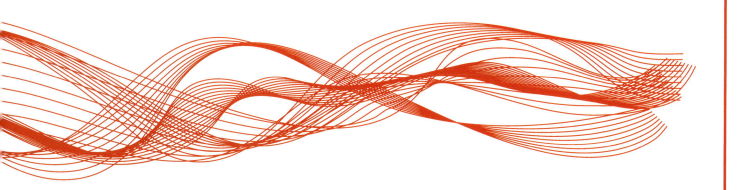

Recorded at Studio Guillaume Tell, Paris, France & Konk Studios, London, England

Produced by David Bascombe & Depeche Mode

Personnel
Dave Gahan
Martin Gore
Andy Fletcher
Alan Wilder

Cover art
Martyn Atkins

Released 28 Sept 1987

Label Mute STUMM 47

Highest chart position on release
UK 10, GER 2, FRA 7, SWE 4, CAN 26, SWI 4, US 35, ITA 7, AUS 60, SPA 1

In the grand tradition of Depeche Mode album releases, its reviews were mixed. Damon Wise of UK weekly music paper *Sounds* gave a tentative thumbs-up to this "missive from the designer doldrums" but Paul Mathur of *Melody Maker* found it "dull." Jane Solanas, aka ex-punk journalist Jane Suck, cut straight to the chase in *NME*.

"What I want to know is, are Depeche Mode pervs?" she pondered. "Their minds are veritable sewers. Leastways Martin Gore's is and the rest of the Modes appear to encourage him, happily singing and playing his bizarre songs.

"Depeche Mode are unashamed pop entertainers and this has been the key to their long success, and the reason why Gore has been able to develop his strange carnal visions and keep the Depeche Mode audience happy."

Enough of the masses liked the album to take it to No. 10 in the UK—slightly lower than its predecessors due to the lack of a big hit single, and their lowest-charting album since *Speak & Spell*—and to No. 2 in Germany. Yet even if their album sales were marking time, touring showed that Depeche Mode were entering the big league.

The *Music for the Masses* tour was to turn into a monster in more ways than one. With fellow Essex synth band Nitzer Ebb in support, it was a mammoth undertaking, with European dates kicking off in October 1987 before a first North American leg leading up to Christmas.

As 1988 opened the band had British dates, including the by-now-obligatory two nights at Wembley, followed by a second jaunt to Europe that incorporated two further trips to Germany, nine arena shows in suddenly infatuated France, and a further venture behind the Iron Curtain. A trip to Japan then led into a final arena-strafing return to North America.

Over an eight-month period, Depeche Mode were to play 101 arena shows—a number that was to acquire significance when the jaunt came to an end.

The first leg of the tour provided yet more evidence that this quirky, deviant band were now serious box office. Close on twenty thousand people packed out each of their three nights at Paris's Omnisports de Paris-Bercy arena. The same number filled the acme

"What I want to know is, are Depeche Mode pervs? Their minds are veritable sewers."

NME

of New York venues, Madison Square Garden, a week before Christmas.

The New Year British dates found critics predictably taking pot shots at the band, with Dave Gahan now firmly in the crosshairs. There was a view that his crowd-pleasing, full-on rock god stage persona was at odds with the introspective gloom of Gore's music.

"Dave Gahan treats us to his fabby new Essex Sex Act," sneered Danny Kelly in *NME*. "We marvel at his convincing pelvis thrusts; we gape at his mastery of the Freddie Mercury aren't-piles-murder? stance; and we stare gobsmacked as (combining the contortions of an arthritic battery hen, a B-movie stripper and Mick Jagger's grandma) he unveils the second worst dance routine on earth."

LEFT The *Music for the Masses* tour arrives in Toronto, Canada, June 1988

ABOVE Essex soulmates and Depeche support band, Nitzer Ebb

> **"I had everything that I could possibly want but I was really lost. I didn't feel like I even knew myself any more."**
> GAHAN

Well used to such mocking dismissals, the prophets without honor in their own land headed to where they were taken more seriously. Before a rare East Berlin show they saw that their appeal crossed over the Wall as ten thousand fans filled the streets hours before the gig in an arena that more usually held the Festival of Political Songs.

The mood on the tour was Bacchanalian, with Martin Gore reprising his on-the-road role of the hard-partying good time that was had by all, while cocaine

joined weed and alcohol on the traditional touring-band menu of downtime distractions. The most marked shift in behavior came from Dave Gahan.

Relatively sober and abstemious on previous tours, Gahan was now beginning to live out a rock-star fantasy both on- and offstage. Sex and drugs and rock and roll, he had clearly decided, were very good indeed—particularly in industrial quantities.

"I had everything that I could possibly want but I was really lost," he was to reflect to *Mojo*, years later. "I didn't feel like I even knew myself any more. And I felt like shit because I constantly cheated on my wife and I went back home and lied."

Gahan's serious decline was yet to come and momentum kept the Depeche party going as it swung across the States in spring '88. This leg of the jaunt was to be documented and chronicled by a major figure from the world of rock documentaries.

Before the US tour began, Mute contacted D. A. Pennebaker, the renowned filmmaker whose career résumé included *Don't Look Back*, the legendary fly-on-the-wall biopic of Bob Dylan's 1965 UK tour. Pennebaker agreed to accompany Depeche across the States and co-direct an on-the-road movie.

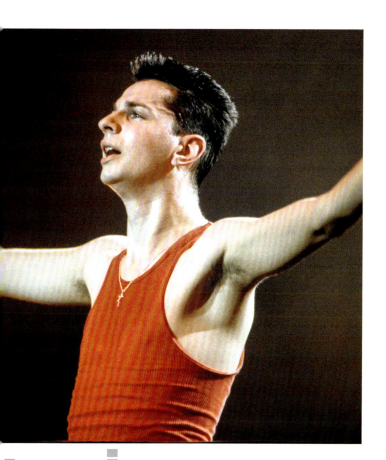

Supported by one of their earliest musical influences, Orchestral Manoeuvres in the Dark, the band weaved across the States, selling out arena after arena. In L.A. they hung out with an unlikely fan in Guns N' Roses singer Axl Rose.

Yet one date was looming large over the touring circus. On June 18, the *Music for the Masses* tour was set to come to a triumphant end at the sixty-thousand-capacity Pasadena Rose Bowl in California. This gigantic show was to form the climax of Pennebaker's documentary—and to lend it its title.

Originally the film was to have been called *Mass*, a play on both *Music for the Masses* and their rapidly multiplying live following. However, when Alan Wilder realized that Pasadena would be the 101st show of the tour, they co-opted this fact for the name of the movie: *101*.

The finished film was a curious, uneven document that nevertheless shone a telling light onto the band's new everyday reality of fame and adulation. Its *cinéma vérité* approach highlighted the thrills, hassles, and tedium at the heart of the vast world tour.

Each band member's personality shone through loud and clear. Gore came over as a shy, self-conscious imp, a grinning, camp *ingénu* in leather shorts who, belying his reputation as a synth-pop obsessive, was rarely glimpsed without his acoustic guitar.

Gahan was by now a force of nature onstage, a pirouetting, animalistic front man who used every Jagger-esque trick in the arena-rock-star book. Clad all in white, he was a charismatic fulcrum for the group, surfing tsunamis of energy from the crowd—yet behind the scenes, cracks were clearly showing.

Telling one US interviewer about a fight he had got into with a taxi driver, Gahan hinted it had been a needed release from the tensions of months of on-the-road life.

"It gets to the point where you could kill someone," he mused, as if thinking aloud. "*I don't think I could do it . . . I'm not sure*. There've been times in the band I've felt possibly I could kill someone. I'd been looking for a fight for a good few days."

Talking to another journalist in another anonymous dressing room, the singer admitted that he was currently not sure life in Depeche Mode was more enjoyable than an earlier, dead-end job stacking supermarket shelves.

"If it's Thursday, this must be . . . party time!"

"You miss your family and you lose all your friends [on the road]," he reflected. "I make a lot more money now than when I worked in the supermarket, but that was more fun."

The permanently semi-amused Wilder appeared the most sorted-out band member, while Fletcher, singing erratic backing vocals behind his synth and dad-dancing with gawky glee, had the air of a man who couldn't quite believe his luck to be in a band touring the world's enormo-domes despite himself possessing only basic musical skills.

"Not much, really," he confessed to an interviewer who asked him what he brought to the group. "My job is to keep everyone together. Martin's the songwriter, Alan's the good musician, Dave's the vocalist, and I . . . bum around."

101 was patchy viewing largely because Pennebaker and his co-directors, David Dawkins and Chris Hegedus, focused on a group of precocious teenage competition-winners making their way by bus across the country to the Rose Bowl gig. As a device, it soon grated: "I could have lived without the 'fans on the bus' angle," Wilder later said.

However, the cameras captured what a thrilling, thrumming electro-machine Depeche Mode live had become. Behind Gahan's wild stage antics lurked a kinetic, brooding musical pulse and a band who were taking stock of just where, and what, their art had brought them to.

In one sweet moment, Gahan and Gore gazed out at sixty thousand disciples in the Rose Bowl then smiled at each other incredulously as they eased into "Behind the Wheel." In another, Gahan waved at a few fans in the crowd—only to find the entire stadium waving back.

"I noticed a couple of people in the audience were sort of waving their arms around so I joined in, and there were suddenly 70,000 people [*sic*] doing that!" he was later to tell *Q* magazine.

"I was just overwhelmed. I kind of felt the tears in me, and sweat rolling down my face, but it was joy. It was like, 'It doesn't get better than this.' It was amazing—Basildon boy makes good!"

"I had very mixed emotions," Daniel Miller said in *Depeche Mode: A Biography*. "When you see 70,000 people doing the same thing at the same time—the

power was really scary. [But] it was incredibly satisfying to see them succeed, against all the odds, really . . . I just wandered around, watching the audience more than the band. It was a very emotional experience."

101 was packed with reminders that Depeche Mode had somehow smoothly morphed into a vast international moneymaking machine. Backstage in Pasadena, Jonathan Kessler, the tour accountant who was eventually to become the band's manager, was counting the cash.

"$1,360,192.50," he marveled to Pennebaker's cameras. "Paid attendance was 60,453 people. We're getting a load of money, a lot of money—tons of money!" Elsewhere in the vast arena, exhausted merchandising staff sat on the concrete floor wielding mountains of dollars.

101 ended with Dave Gahan, looking like a white-clad stick insect, crouched on a catwalk, cheerleading and conducting a crowd that stretched as far as the eye could see through "Everything Counts." The next morning, Depeche Mode piled from a stretch limo into their waiting private jet to fly home.

It was beginning to look as if it must be hugely exhilarating and very lonely up there.

> **"You miss your family and you lose all your friends. I make a lot more money now than when I worked in the supermarket, but that was more fun."**
>
> **GAHAN**

Dave Gahan at the Pasadena Rose Bowl, June 1988: "I miss stacking shelves . . ."

7
IMMACULATE VIOLATION

Daniel Miller knew that Depeche Mode had crossed the Rubicon in Pasadena. The weirdo Essex cult electronic band had filled a US venue beyond the reach of all but the most populist of rock bands.

"I think the Rose Bowl concert had a huge influence on people's perception of the band and, to be honest, we made sure that it did," he later admitted. "It was a massive leap of vision for them to decide to play there and the fact that it sold out instantly was incredible."

Back in London, Miller could hardly believe it had happened—but he wanted to make the most of it. To that end, he decided the release of Pennebaker's *101* documentary the following March would be accompanied with a live album of the same name.

Determined to stress Depeche's heightened international status and counter their negative image at home, he also hired a new UK press person to work closely with the band. Mick Paterson joined Mute in June 1988 as head of promotion.

"The week that I started, everybody else at Mute had disappeared to Pasadena for the Rose Bowl show," he recalls. "So, I sat down to read their massive

"You were either in the Erasure camp— if you'll pardon the pun—or the Depeche camp. It was quite divided like that."

PATERSON

UK press file and it didn't read well. I thought, *My God, how are we going to turn this around?*

"The British press write-ups were all very snide and dismissive. They were all making fun of them coming from Basildon, or the way that Martin used to dress. There was no acknowledgment of what they were doing musically at all."

Paterson also became aware of a hangover within the record label of the band's early divorce from Vince Clarke. "Erasure were becoming really successful in Britain at the time and it always felt within Mute that there was competition between the two bands," he says.

"You were either in the Erasure camp—if you'll pardon the pun—or the Depeche camp. It was quite divided like that. There were big fans of Erasure in the office who weren't that keen on Depeche, and vice versa."

Paterson's strategy to try to fix Depeche Mode's domestic image was to stress their international standing—and influence. He knew the band had been lauded by underground DJs and producers on the then-nascent US techno scene such as Kevin Saunderson (the Inner City man who had described "Get the Balance Right" as "the first ever house record"), Juan Atkinson, and Frankie Knuckles.

"When it came time to promote *101*, I said, 'Why don't we just do one big interview?'" he says.

PREVIOUS PAGE Dave Gahan on stage in Rotterdam, 1990

"Whose camp are you in?" Dave Gahan (far left) and Erasure (left)

"*The Face* [a now-defunct UK monthly style/culture magazine] was all over the house music and Ecstasy scene and was a very credible thing to be in.

"The band were reluctant to talk to the UK press because of all their bad experiences but if they found a journalist they felt comfortable with, they were good interviewees. So, we flew to Detroit with John McCready from *The Face*, who was into both techno and Depeche."

The trip was an eye-opener for the band. Having stopped off in New York to watch Pennebaker doing the final edit of *101*, they flew on to Detroit, where Paterson and *The Face* had arranged for them to meet techno pioneer and guru Derrick May.

"I asked May to come to our hotel but he told me, 'No, you have to come to my apartment,'" says Paterson. "So, we were all going to his flat and I remember a couple of the band were saying, 'Who the fuck *is* Derrick May, anyway?'"

Band opinion on May was to be divided. While Fletcher found him a "really nice bloke," Alan Wilder begged to differ: "He was horrible: I hated him. He was the most arrogant fucker I ever met," he later shuddered. However, the night took a spectacular upturn when May took the band to a nearby house club in a disused church, The Music Institute.

"It was the time when Detroit city centre was a complete vacuum because everybody had moved out," says Paterson. "It was bleak and cold and snowing. We all needed security at the club and when we got there we had to wait in the van because somebody had been shot outside."

Yet when Depeche got inside the club it was a revelation. They found that they were idolized by the Institute's achingly hip, predominantly black young clientele who had been dancing for months to the music of this exotic, unknown white European synth band.

In characteristic style, Depeche Mode were both delighted and dumbfounded by this unexpected development.

"We got mobbed by all these pretty young black kids!" a perplexed Fletcher was to report. Gore was equally mystified, telling McCready: "We can't create dance music and I don't think we have ever really tried. We honestly wouldn't know where to start." Gahan was even more forthright: "Our music is as white as it comes, very European and not made for dancing."

Their lack of knowledge of the techno/Ecstasy scene extended to being miffed that the Music Institute did not serve alcohol. Comically baffled prophets they may have been but the Detroit trip was proof of the group's under-celebrated influence on electronic music. When the next issue of *The Face* appeared, the magazine's cover line posed an explosive question:

DID DEPECHE MODE DETONATE HOUSE?

"Suddenly they went from being these weird S&M characters that nobody took seriously to being the band that started house music!" says Paterson.

"The piece said the guys in Detroit were taking their inspiration from Kraftwerk and other white European

Dave Gahan in 1989; detonating the house music explosion?

bands such as Depeche. It made some people in Britain think, 'Oh, they're cooler than we thought.'"

Mission accomplished—for a while, at least. Pennebaker's *101* movie was critically well received, and the accompanying live record even outperformed *Music for the Masses* in the UK, charting at No. 5.

Martin Gore indulged himself in a little extracurricular activity, recording a solo EP of cover versions, *Counterfeit*. Released by Mute in June, it featured Gore takes on favorite tracks by left-field artists as various as Tuxedomoon, Durutti Column, and Comsat Angels, plus a spectral version of Sparks' "Never Turn Your Back on Mother Earth."

This was a mere amuse-bouche, though. By now it was time to begin work on a new Depeche Mode album—the one that was to blow the world wide open for them.

With Dave Bascombe working with Tears For Fears and unavailable, Depeche cast around for a new co-producer. Early in 1989 At Daniel Miller's behest, they settled on one Mark "Flood" Ellis, a tyro studio engineer who was fast making a name for himself.

Flood had worked on U2's *The Joshua Tree* blockbuster with Brian Eno and Daniel Lanois before then moving on to Depeche Mode's labelmates/nemesis Erasure's second album, *The Circus*. This prime experience of both elite rock and pop made him an attractive proposition for the genre-straddling band.

His initial impression, nevertheless, was somewhat underwhelming: "This scruffy, bespectacled, rather unlikely-looking bloke rolled up," Wilder was to report. "He raided the fridge, slouched down on the sofa, pontificated for a bit, and thus—a new production team was born."

Wilder and Flood were to be the main production duo on the album that was to become *Violator*, and after a short, exploratory session in London they flew with the rest of the band to Milan to work in Logic Studios. One early song that Martin Gore had packed in his luggage excited everybody.

When Gore presented "Personal Jesus" to the rest of the band, it was little more than a beat, allied to a melody played on his ubiquitous acoustic guitar. The potential at the heart of the tune struck them all immediately.

Dave Gahan, an unlikely cock-rocker

"We loved it," Andy Fletcher was to inform *Uncut*, years later. "We thought it was a great song, great sound . . . We also thought [because of the lyrical content], *this song is not going to get played at all.*"

"Personal Jesus" played Gore's usual lyrical trick of melding the sacred and the sexual, the pious and the profane, but this time he went that little bit . . . further. "*Reach out and touch faith!*" its rich opening urged, as Gahan promised to be ". . . *someone to hear your prayers/Someone who cares.*" Gore was later to admit the song had been inspired by reading in Priscilla Presley's autobiography about how much she had worshipped Elvis.

Flood and Wilder mixed up a storm around the track, weaving its main synthesized glam-rock stomp from samples of people jumping up and down on flight cases in the recording studio. Depeche knew they had come up with something special . . . but would it be in vain?

"We thought that, especially in America, it might struggle for airplay," Gore was to confess, years later. "We were proven totally wrong."

Released as an early taster of *Violator* in August 1989, the louche rhythms of "Personal Jesus" seduced radio programmers on both sides of the Atlantic. It was also helped by an unorthodox, left-field promotional gimmick.

"A marketing guy thought up a great campaign," remembers Mick Paterson. "It was before the internet, so we placed personal ads in newspapers: *Do you need your own Personal Jesus?* It had an

0800 number, and when people called up they got a clip of the song."

Another major boost was provided by a moody, Anton Corbijn-directed mock-spaghetti-Western video, shot in Spain, which won over MTV. "Personal Jesus" hit No. 13 in the UK and No. 28 in the US—their highest chart placing Stateside since 1984's "People Are People."

Heartened by this success, the band returned to Denmark's Puk Studios, where they had remixed *Music for the Masses*, to pick up work on *Violator*. The album began to come together fairly quickly but one band member was feeling notably detached from its genesis.

With his talents lying in organization and administration rather than musical abilities, Andy Fletcher could sometimes feel cut adrift in the studio, where he had little to contribute on the writing or production side. Always a twitchy, highly strung figure, he sank into a profound depression in Denmark.

Fletch was later to identify the cause as delayed grieving for his sister, Karen, who had died of cancer four years earlier. Its symptoms took the form of imagining himself to be suffering from a string of serious ailments. His concerned bandmates persuaded him to fly home and check into the Priory (where he found himself beginning his recovery alongside Lol Tolhurst of the Cure).

Fletcher's absence had no great creative impact on the recording of *Violator*, for which Gore was continuing to come up with exceptional material. "Policy of Truth" unfolded around a skittering rhythmic skein, with malign menace; "World in My Eyes" brooded in sultry, mildly kinky style: "Let my hands do the soothing."

Strongest of all, though, was "Enjoy the Silence," which opened with a New Order-like guitar shimmer before swooping into a poetic reverie on the nature of infatuation: *"Words are very unnecessary/They can only do harm."* Dave Gahan's velvet drawl husked the words as if they were the purest gospel.

By the time the band transferred to the Eurythmics' Dave Stewart's Church Studios in north London to complete and mix *Violator*, they knew they had a special album on their hands. When they presented it to their US and UK labels, Daniel Miller and Seymour Stein felt exactly the same.

"Their promotions guy in America, Bruce Kirkland, organized an album signing in a shopping mall in Los Angeles," says Paterson. "He expected about 1,000 people. More than 17,000 turned up and it became a bit of a riot. Security had to close the whole mall down."

"Enjoy The Silence" charted at No. 6 in the UK, Depeche Mode's most successful single since "People Are People" six years earlier, and was similarly successful across the globe. It was a No. 8 hit in the US, where it also topped Billboard's Modern Rock chart.

Europe certainly took the track to its heart. "Enjoy The Silence" was to go Top 5 in Germany, Finland, Ireland, Sweden and Switzerland, as well as hitting No. 1 in reliably devoted Spain. In Italy, this sultry, sexily understated murmur of a song was to become the band's first platinum single in any territory.

Possibly as an after-effect of the realization that this band could fill sixty-thousand-seater American stadia, UK reviews of *Violator* were more positive than usual when it appeared in March 1990. *Melody Maker* praised it as the band's "most arresting work to date," while *NME* noted that it was dealing with "raw emotions . . . big subjects that can be hard to capture in a three-minute pop song."

For some critics, though, old habits died hard. *Sounds* reverted to type by mocking their "lyrical naivety" and "child-like artlessness." "If William Burroughs wrote for Gahan, Depeche Mode would be terrifying," it claimed. "But he doesn't. Martin Gore writes for Gahan and Depeche Mode are hilarious."

"The press was still a little bit snitty," confirms Mick Paterson, who was fast becoming resigned to that fate. "The reviews for *Violator* weren't universally amazing. That bothered the band because, like most

Andy Fletcher was to succumb to a deep depression

groups, when they read their reviews it's always the worst one that sticks with them."

"Journalists have always had a go at Martin about his lyrics, and I think that he would admit that he's not Kafka. But I bet Depeche Mode have sold more records than Kafka ever sold books."

American critics were also somewhat lukewarm. *Rolling Stone* felt Gahan sounded "slimy and self-involved" and complained that the band "revert to morose pop psychology [but] never tell you how come they're so sad." This was at odds with *Spin*, who lauded the album for having, somehow, "caught the American nation's mood of dread, doubt and uncertainty."

By now, however, Depeche Mode fans did not scrutinize reviews to decide whether to buy their albums. They raced out to record shops on the day of release. *Violator* powered to No. 2 in the UK, kept off the top by Phil Collins's saccharine monstrosity . . . *But Seriously*. In the US it hit No. 7 en route to going triple-platinum.

"Reach out and touch faith . . ." It was time, yet again, for Depeche Mode to go out and entertain the ever-increasing hordes who put such faith in them.

The band went into the vast *World Violation* tour with their front man in an emotional state of flux. Dave Gahan had recently left his wife, Jo, and young son, Jack, after a difficult few months. Ironically, his attempts to seek help through this marital minefield had led him to a new partner.

Gahan had got into the habit of long, soul-searching transatlantic phone calls with Teresa Conroy, the

Depechemode

violator

"[*Violator*] has caught the
American nation's mood of dread,
doubt and uncertainty."

SPIN

Violator

TRACK LIST

World in My Eyes
Sweetest Perfection
Personal Jesus
Halo
Waiting for The Night

Enjoy the Silence / Interlude #2
(Crucified)
Policy of Truth
Blue Dress / Interlude #3
Clean

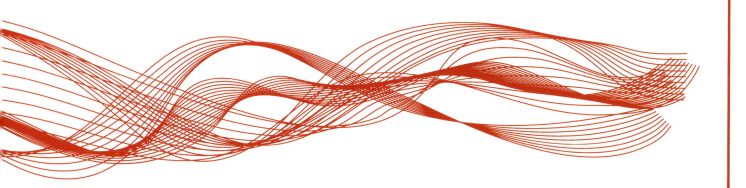

Recorded at Logic, Milan, Italy, Puk, Gjerlev, Denmark; The Church and Master Rock, London, England and Axis, New York, USA

Produced by Flood & Depeche Mode

Personnel
Dave Gahan
Martin Gore
Andy Fletcher
Alan Wilder

Cover art
Anton Corbijn

Released 19 Mar 1990

Label Mute CD STUMM 64

Highest chart position on release
UK 2, GER 2, FRA 1, SWE 6, CAN 5, SWI 2, US 7, ITA 6, AUS 42, SPA 1

> **"Then all of a sudden, I discovered heroin, and I'd be lying if I said it didn't make me feel . . . *like I've never felt before.* I felt like I really belonged."**
>
> GAHAN

band's US press representative who had played a cameo role in Pennebaker's *101*. When they met up again in person for *World Violation*, they became an item.

The tour was a massive undertaking, with a huge stage set featuring monochrome imagery by Anton Corbijn projected onto vast screens. The band again traveled between shows by private jet as eleven articulated trucks lumbered after them, manned by a hundred tour staff.

The ticket sales for the opening forty-four-date North American leg were prodigious. Depeche had never before played in Florida. Now they began the tour in May 1990 with four dates in Pensacola, Orlando, Miami, and Tampa to a total of forty-five thousand people.

The bigger the arena or stadium, the quicker it sold out. Amazingly, forty-two thousand tickets for New York's Giants Stadium went inside four hours. Dallas's twenty-thousand-capacity Starplex Amphitheatre sold out immediately. When they added a second night, it did the same. They racked up no less than three nights at San Diego's Sports Arena.

Most astonishing of all, forty-eight thousand tickets for the US leg's closing date at Los Angeles's Dodger Stadium were snapped up as soon as they went on sale. It could have been seen as the band chancing their luck when they added a second show, but no—that sold out, too.

Depeche Mode were now firmly on the stadium-zonking world-tour treadmill only trodden by the most elevated rock superstars. It was an itinerary up there with the Rolling Stones, Springsteen, and Bon Jovi. Years later, Alan Wilder was to detail a typical day on the *World Violation* tour.

"Check out of hotel at 1pm or 2pm," he recalled to UK music writer Stephen Dalton. "Travel to local airfield. Fly by private jet with the immediate entourage (about 12 people) to the next city. Arrive 4pm approx. Go straight to the gig for soundcheck.

"Back to the hotel at 6pm, quick sauna/workout, if there was time, leave for the gig at 7.45pm. Onstage 8.30pm/9pm: offstage 11pm, followed by hospitality and night on the town until the early hours . . . repeat 44 times!"

It was a classic on-the-road hermetic bubble at the heart of the wild excess of a multi-million-dollar-grossing rock and roll tour. Insulated from reality, the band partied hard, with cocaine and Ecstasy joining the band's staple tour diet of lakes of lager. "Ecstasy was the thing, and you'd pop an E after every show," Gahan was to say, years later.

The Depeche Mode singer was to take things even further, though. Wracked by guilt at leaving his wife and son and partying hard with his new partner and soulmate, Teresa Conroy, he turned to heroin.

"I'd been drinking and using drugs for a long time, probably since I was 12," he was to tell *Q* years later, as he reviewed a lifetime's narcotic intake. "Popping a couple of Mum's phenobarbitones every now and then. Hash. Amphetamines. Coke came along. Alcohol was always there, hand in hand with drugs.

"Then, all of a sudden, I discovered heroin, and I'd be lying if I said it didn't make me feel . . . *like I've never felt before*. I felt like I really belonged. I felt nothing was going to hurt me. I was invincible. That was the euphoria. From the moment I first injected, I wanted to feel like that all the time."

After entertaining close on 100,000 over two nights at the Dodger Stadium, Depeche flew on to Australia, then did six nights in Japan, including two at the Budokan. The final three months of 1990 were spent touring European arenas; the demand for British dates was mopped up by three nights each at Wembley and Birmingham NEC. By the time *World Violation* was over, Depeche Mode had played to almost one-and-a-quarter million people.

So, how were they going to follow *that*?

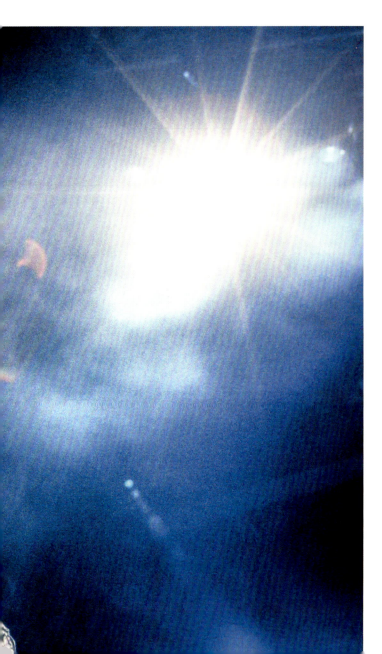

The *World Violation* tour hits Tokyo, 1990

8

"THE MOST DEBAUCHED TOUR EVER"

nitially, they did nothing at all.

World Violation had been a draining tour and the majority of the band went to ground to lick their wounds. Forever the inseparable duo, Fletcher and Gore both became fathers, the former with his long-term partner, Gráinne, the latter with Texan girlfriend Suzanne Boisvert, whom he had met in Paris two years earlier.

Just before the birth of Gore's daughter, Viva Lee, his mother finally revealed the true story of his parentage. Pamela Gore told her son he was the result of a short relationship she had with an American GI stationed in Britain from 1960 to 1961—who was black.

This came as a considerable shock to Gore. He has rarely talked about it publicly, but on a future trip to the US he managed to track down and meet his African-American biological father. It was reportedly an awkward encounter.

Going by a blog post written in March 2012 by an American music fan, Miles Goosens, this meeting will have probably taken place in Bland County, Virginia. On his Reading Pronunciation blog, Goosen wrote

of having a relative who lived in this remote corner of the Appalachians and worked at a local shop that made electrical items such as large generator parts for factories.

The sole non-white employee in this shop was a middle-aged black janitor who, incongruously, always wore a Depeche Mode baseball cap. Goosen's relative one day jokingly asked his co-worker about this unlikely headwear. He did not expect the answer he got.

"My son is Martin Gore," the janitor told him.

During the hiatus from Depeche, Alan Wilder married his girlfriend, Jeri Young. He also recorded a new Recoil album, this time with a clutch of guest vocalists: Moby, Toni Halliday of Curve, and Doug McCarthy of Nitzer Ebb.

PREVIOUS PAGE Dave Gahan on stage at Oakland Coliseum, California, USA on November 12, 1993

LEFT Dave Gahan in rock god mode

BELOW Martin Gore tracked down his biological dad

One member of Depeche Mode, however, was not taking time out to reflect and repair. With nowhere to go back to after his marital split from Jo, Dave Gahan upped sticks and moved to America, where he set up home in Los Angeles with his new partner, Teresa Conroy. He took to his new home city rather too well.

Gahan's taste for the rock and roll lifestyle had grown through the *Music for the Masses* and *World Violation* tours. Relocated to the City of Angels, with no family or young son to hold him back, and with a willing playmate in Conroy, Gahan began to say yes to a new excess on a daily basis.

Depeche Mode may have begun life as an all-electronic, anti-rock-cliché entity, but within Dave Gahan had always lurked a frustrated rock star, a man who longed to pout and move like Jagger, Mercury, or Morrison. Living in L.A., he had every chance to act out this fantasy.

"I actually consciously thought, *There's no fucking rock stars out there anymore*," he was to confess to *NME*'s Keith Cameron. "There's nobody willing to *go the whole way* to do this. So, what's missing? What's needed here? What am I missing?

"It's one thing singing the songs, but does anybody really *mean* it? So, I created a monster. I made the mistake of thinking that *meaning* it meant you had to take yourself to the very depths of hell. So, I dragged my body through the mud, to show that I could do it."

Musically, Gahan fell in love with the macho, testosterone-heavy rock then being pumped out of L.A.—the decadent Jane's Addiction, the socially woke Rage Against the Machine—as well as grunge rock bands such as Nirvana, Pearl Jam, and Alice in Chains. His appearance began to reflect his new predilection.

Egged on by his rock-chick soulmate, Gahan began sporting Eddie Vedder shoulder-length hair and a hipster goatee, riding a Harley Davidson and gaining tattoos: a Celtic dagger here, a Hindu symbol there. Beneath a love heart on his forearm were the letters "TCTTM-FG": an acronym for "Teresa Conroy To The Mother-Fucking Gahan."

These were arguably harmless affectations. Gahan's increased drug use was a more serious matter. Together with Conroy, he set off on a path of Sid-and-Nancy-style heroin-led narcotic excess that within weeks led to the singer looking a wasted, emaciated mess.

Looking, in fact, what he was—a junkie.

Gahan had zero contact with the rest of Depeche Mode throughout 1991. However, on a few sporadic visits to London to see his son, Jack, he met up with Daniel Miller at Mute.

Miller, who had been around rock bands for fifteen years and worked for many years with Nick Cave, knew what Gahan had become as soon as he saw him.

"I hadn't seen him for a few months and he looked a classic junkie," he told Steve Malins in *Depeche Mode: A Biography*. "He was skinny, he looked terrible, and that was when I knew he was a junkie.

"He used to do this great impression of a wasted rock star and here he was—he'd *become* that impersonation, even down to the fact that his problem was so obvious but he was trying to conceal it from me."

"He used to do this great impression of a wasted rock star and here he was— he'd *become* that impersonation."

MILLER

Rock and roll influences on Dave Gahan: Jane's Addiction (left) and Rage Against the Machine (below)

In this parlous state and cocooned with Conroy in L.A., Gahan was by no means sure he wanted to continue with Depeche Mode. Their sophisticated, pristine machine music was alien to his current state of mind. Then, at the end of 1991, Martin Gore called him up.

Gore told his singer he had written a few demos for the next album. When Gahan received the disks, and heard early versions of "I Feel You" and "Condemnation," he was delighted to hear they were far bluesier and rockier than expected.

"It was a total relief!" he was to confess, years later. "I was so glad Martin was moving away from the dance-music formula. When he started sending me bluesy demos for the new record, I thought, 'Great!' In fact, I looked in a mirror and started playing air guitar!"

After their year apart, Depeche Mode agreed to reconvene in Madrid in January 1992 to start work on their next album. It was the first time the other three saw what Gahan had changed into: *what he*

had become. They could not conceal their horror.

"I had changed, but I didn't really understand it until I came face to face with Al and Mart and Fletch," Gahan was to tell *Q* magazine in 1997. "The looks on their faces . . . battered me."

Gahan was a changed man . . . and yet Alan Wilder was later to reflect that the transformation had been expected.

"To be honest, it wasn't too much of a shock when we saw Dave in Madrid," he told Steve Malins in *Depeche Mode: A Biography*. "We were all expecting it. We knew, given how he'd seemed the last time we saw him, and the fact that he'd been living in L.A., that he'd come back different.

"I think Dave is very, very easily influenced. He's a vulnerable kind of character and he goes to extremes. So, it wasn't surprising . . . but it was a bit saddening."

Relations within the band were strained and about to get worse. Depeche Mode's previous attempt to make an album in intense, claustrophobic conditions, 1986's *Black Celebration*, had been a disaster. They were about to repeat the mistake.

Fresh from working on U2's *Achtung Baby*, which saw them spend weeks in each other's pockets in Berlin, producer Flood wanted to apply the same methodology to Depeche. The band thus rented a villa thirty miles out of Madrid and turned it into a residential studio.

"It was in this really odd location on the outskirts of the city, like a gated estate, the sort of place where Costa del Crime people live," Daniel Miller was to reflect. "Very high security, big houses, beautiful gardens . . . but sort of weird."

Flood booked the band in to work in Madrid for two initial six-week sessions, with a month's break in between. It quickly became clear that communal living, given how estranged everyone currently felt, was hugely ambitious. Miller could see something was wrong when he arrived:

> It was obvious what the problem was. They'd spent time apart, they'd all gone through quite big changes in their lives, some of them had had kids in that period, and there wasn't

that natural coming together any more.

I walked into the house [a week into the recording sessions] and it was the worst vibe. Everyone seemed to be in their own little space and nobody was relating to each other at all. Alan was in the drum room, just drumming away to himself. Dave was locked in his room, painting . . . Fletch and Mart were reading the *Sun*.

It's not an untypical scene in a studio but usually it's three months in, not one week. You'd expect a bustle of activity but it felt like they had burned out before they'd even started.

Fixated on Jane's Addiction and Alice in Chains, Gahan was insisting the album needed a rockier, edgier feel. Gore was feeling pressure to write songs as commercial as those on *Violator*. Fletcher continued to struggle with depression and confidence issues.

As the album's main producers, Flood and Wilder agreed on a more organic, live feel to the recordings. Slowly, painfully, songs began to come together. "Condemnation" and "Walking in My Shoes"

Gahan (left) wanted Depeche to channel Alice in Chains (right)

"I was so 'out there' that I didn't notice anything. I would come down sporadically with bursts of creative emotion, then I'd go back to my room again."

GAHAN

emerged from that most un-Depeche Mode-like of activities: in-studio jam sessions.

Singing alone in the villa's garage, Gahan provided a tremendous vocal for the former, and his contributions were to be driven but erratic. Frequently, he absented himself to his room to paint, or to feed white noise from his guitar into an amp.

"Dave had clearly deteriorated," Alan Wilder was later to reflect. "He occasionally surfaced to sing a couple of takes or offer a few words of encouragement, and then he'd disappear again."

"I was so 'out there' that I didn't notice *anything*," Gahan was later to confess, with his customary beguiling honesty. "I was painting in my room. I would come down sporadically with bursts of creative emotion, then I'd go back to my room again."

It was a relief for all parties when the mid-recording break came around. Gahan flew back to L.A. and in April married his partner-in-sin, Teresa Conroy, at the Graceland Chapel in Las Vegas, serenaded by an Elvis impersonator.

When the band met up again a couple of weeks later in Hamburg, they were a man down. Andy Fletcher had found the tense Madrid sessions unbearable. Never an essential musical component of the band, he skipped the sessions and stayed behind in London.

Germany was to prove more productive than had Spain. Gahan, Gore, and Wilder might be jamming now but the technology and studio trickery that Flood was applying to tracks such as "Mercy in

You" and "Judas" left them sounding like definitive Depeche Mode.

Finishing off the album, at Olympic Studios in London, Flood even drafted in a gospel trio to sing on the haltingly euphoric "Get Right with Me." Gore confessed to severe misgivings about the idea, then had a spiritual epiphany: "The moment that they started singing, it lifted the track on to another level."

Dave Gahan was by now the main walking-wounded casualty of Depeche Mode but all of the band were clearly nursing effects of their riotously hedonistic lifestyle. Around this time, I was to discover this for myself during a bizarre chance encounter in the unlikely setting of a B&B bar in Minehead, Somerset.

I was attending the wedding of a mutual friend, Steev Toth, a music industry soundman and tour manager who knew Depeche well. At the end of a long and lively day, I wandered into my B&B with a friend at 3am to discover three intrepid figures still up and drinking in the semi-dark bar.

It was Gore, Fletcher, and Wilder, and they summoned the two of us over to their table.

"Come over here," instructed Gore, "and be our moral budgies."

We joined them. Pardon? Moral budgies?

"He means judges," explained the grinning Wilder.

Gore fixed me with a somewhat pie-eyed stare. "What it is," he began, "is that I've taken a lot of drugs over the years, right? A lot of drugs. But I've never been . . . brain-affected. I'm not. Am I?"

It seemed that his fellow band members had been suggesting that prolonged enthusiastic narcotic ingestion tended to compromise mental efficiency. It felt hard to deliver a snap verdict on Gore's own faculties on the spot, but I assured him that, at that moment, he appeared lucid and *compos mentis*. Satisfied with my answer, Gore slumped back in his chair as I began talking to Fletcher and Wilder.

Two minutes later, I felt a tug at my sleeve. It seemed Gore was feeling the need to return to our previous topic.

"That's the thing, you see," he said. "I've taken a lot of drugs in my life so far . . ." he trailed away slightly, ". . . but I'm not brain-affected!"

I once more expressed my agreement with this statement—only to be asked again two minutes later.

"Dave had clearly deteriorated . . ." - Alan Wilder

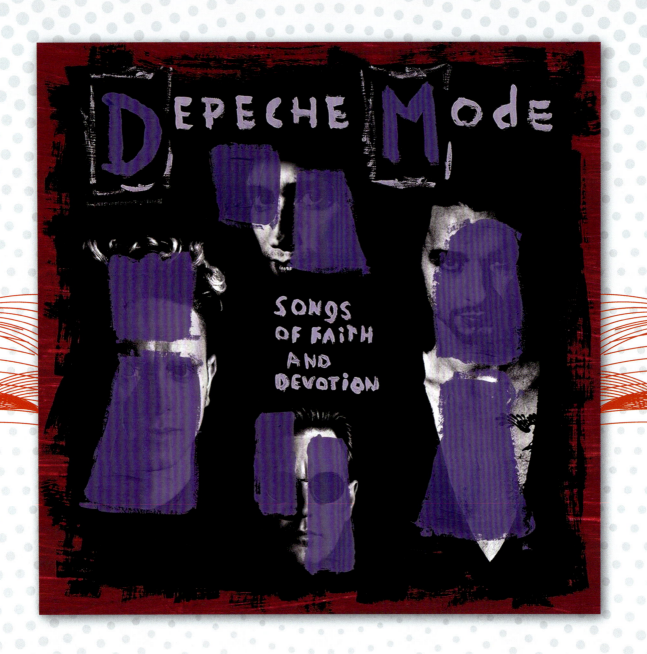

"The songs make desire more desperate,
and more alluring, than ever."

NEW YORK TIMES

Songs of Faith and Devotion

TRACK LIST

I Feel You

Walking in My Shoes

Condemnation

Mercy in You

Judas

In Your Room

Get Right with Me / Interlude #4

Rush

One Caress

Higher Love

Recorded at Chateau Du Pape, Hamburg, Germany and villa studio, Madrid Spain

Produced by Flood & Depeche Mode

Personnel
Dave Gahan
Martin Gore
Andy Fletcher
Alan Wilder

Cover art
Anton Corbijn

Released 22 Mar 1993

Label Mute CD STUMM 106

Highest chart position on release
UK 1, GER 1, FRA 1, SWE 2, CAN 5, SWI 1, US 1, ITA 6, AUS 14, SPA 2

This bizarre conversational motif repeated itself over the following thirty minutes until this particular moral budgie gave up, called it a night, and headed off to bed, leaving the Mode trio still quaffing downstairs. Thankfully, it seemed, totally non-brain-affected.

The making of the record that became *Songs of Faith and Devotion* had been thorny. Flood was to call it the "hardest album he had ever made" and declare it was his last record with the band: "I didn't want to put myself through all *that* again!" But somehow, at the end of it all, there was a new Depeche Mode album to savor.

Songs of Faith and Devotion was a sleek, malign, troubled hum—Flood was to call it "dark, very dark"—and reviewers lauded its depth and intensity. Nodding towards the Flood/Corbijn U2 connections in *NME*, David Quantick called it "an album that out-*Achtung Babys Achtung Baby* . . . an album every sane person should own."

In the US, the *New York Times* reflected that "the songs make desire more desperate, and more alluring, than ever." Forever faintly sniffy towards synth bands, *Rolling Stone* was more equivocal about the album: "like the band itself, it's gloomy, pretentious and winning."

They could have declared the record less authentic than Milli Vanilli and it would not have impacted its sales. Released on March 22 in Britain, and a day later in America, *Songs of Faith and Devotion* made its way to No. 1 in both countries—as well as in Germany, France, Italy, etc, etc.

Now, it was time to take it on the road.

The *Devotional* tour was scheduled to kick off in Lille, France in May 1993 before wending its way across Europe until the end of July. A fifty-date North American fall tour would then lead into pre-Christmas shows back in the UK.

Spending months on its conception, Anton Corbijn had designed an elaborate stage set on two levels. Raised at the back, Gore, Fletcher, and Wilder would bleep keyboards in front of eleven enormous video screens of gnomic, abstract imagery: down below them, prowling an empty space, Dave Gahan would do his ultimate-rock-star shtick.

The *Devotional* tour was to be a huge global enterprise and at least half of the band were in no

Acting out his 'ultimate-rock-star-shtick': Dave Gahan

LEFT Martin Gore
RIGHT Andy Fletcher
FAR RIGHT Dave Gahan
BELOW Depeche Mode
live in London, 1993

state to undertake it. Despite having married Gráinne on January 16, Andy Fletcher remained nervy and fragile. His black dog was straining at its leash.

Gahan had a huge, winged tattoo of a protective angel tattooed on his upper back, and did intensive circuit training to get himself into shape for the tour, but within the camp he was fooling nobody. His rampant drug habit remained—and the road was no place to take it.

Gahan's heroin addiction was the main reason that the 120-strong *Devotional* staff entourage included a psychiatrist whom they were reportedly paying $4,000 per week.

"The idea was that he could provide some kind of support for those who wanted it, although the real reason was to try to persuade Dave to come off the smack, because we weren't confident he was going to make it to the end of the tour," Alan Wilder later admitted.

"Ironically, I think everyone went to see the shrink at some point—except Dave, who was far too wise to the scheme!"

Gahan was also wise enough, even in the throes of addiction, to see that the *Devotional* tour would be "like taking a mental asylum on the road." In later years, *Q* magazine was to bestow upon the jaunt the dubious plaudit of "The Most Debauched Tour Ever."

When it kicked off in May, it was clear the show was on two different levels in every way. As Gore, Fletcher, and Wilder gazed down impassively from above, Gahan threw himself around his gladiatorial pit like an emaciated Iggy Pop. Gore and Wilder came down only to play live guitar and drums, respectively, on "I Feel You."

Offstage Gahan was a recluse, secluded in his own dressing room, a cavern of Keith Richards-style drapes and candles. The tour party felt sure he was shooting up in there but nobody—including Jonathan Kessler, by now promoted from accountant to tour manager—felt able to intercede.

Nor were the rest of the party united. Alan Wilder was often irritated by the bluff, non-musical Fletcher, and this appeared to be hardening into an active dislike. Gahan and Wilder both traveled to shows in separate limos; Gore and Fletcher arrived in a third.

On a flying visit to the tour, Daniel Miller saw that intra-band tensions were worse even than they had been in Madrid.

"It was different limos, different hotel floors," he reflected, years later. "I don't think anyone spoke to Dave the entire tour. They saw Dave on stage and then he went off into his dressing room and his candles and everything.

"Alan wasn't really talking to Martin and Fletch. Obviously, it was very sad in some ways. But if you saw the funny side, the ridiculous side, it was *Spinal Tap*, too."

Journalists who flew out to the tour returned home with lurid tales of a mobile Sodom and Gomorrah. They talked of a barely *compos mentis* Gahan hanging out with drug dealers; of sex-themed post-show parties; of roadies hand-picking the most beautiful girls in the crowd to be taken to the Mode's lair.

Spiritualized, the tour's support band, went down badly at the first few dates and were junked. When they were replaced by fellow Mute signings Miranda Sex Garden, that band's violinist Hepzibah Sessa formed a close friendship with the married Wilder.

Despite the hostile backstage atmosphere, *Devotional* was going down a storm, routinely selling out sports arenas and stadiums. In Mannheim in June, Dave Gahan took his rock messiah pose a step further and dived headfirst into the crowd.

"It's scary, it's a weird thing with all these hands, a million hands all over you, pulling you," he said. "You see faces and suddenly you see someone like one of our security guards and they're, like, 'Dave, we've got you.' They ripped my shirt off."

Gahan was to use his mauling by fans as a cover for the scars wending their way up his upper arms. The wider world had long suspected, but the *Devotional* tour was to be when his drug addiction was finally made public.

Back in London, *NME* asked Depeche's press agent, Mick Paterson, if one of their writers, Gavin Martin, could join the tour to write a front-page cover story. Paterson agreed but was wary from the off.

"The band were very reluctant to talk to the *NME* but the label and I persuaded them to do it—after all, it was a cover," he says. "So, Gavin and I flew out in July to meet the tour in Budapest.

"The *NME* was always a pain in the arse, and even on the flight out I was regretting the fact that Gavin was doing it. He was clearly only going out there to dig up dirt. I could tell nothing good was going to come of it."

Backstage at Budapest's Hidegkuti Nándor Stadium, Martin entered Gahan's den, which he then described in incredulous terms in *NME*: "Gahan's own private dressing room has been transformed into a darkened cavern. Candles burn on table-tops, on flight cases and other surfaces provided by his makeshift, on-the-road furniture.

"Loud music blasts from his hi-fi, jasmine incense sticks are burned to give the atmosphere he desires. Behind him there's a red carpet hung against the wall . . . a full rock 'n' roll Parnassian set-up. Such are the trappings that befit a Cool Icon, a man playing—or trying to play—the role of A Rock God."

Nor did Martin stint on his description of Gahan himself. "He doesn't look or sound like a well man," he reported. "His skin is sickly grey in the half light,

his eyes sunk into blueish sockets. Beneath his vest, tattoos embellish his biceps and torso but the insides of his long skinny arms are all bruised and scratched.

"His 'problems' have become Depeche Mode's dirty little secret—everybody in the camp knows about them. Gahan talks about them in vague terms. He means to get them 'sorted out,' he says. But everyone knows a rock 'n' roll tour isn't really the place to start sorting things out."

It was a devastating exposé that realized all of Paterson's worst fears on the flight over. He was disgusted. "That article was a snide-y piece of shit,"

Dave Gahan: "His 'problems' have become Depeche Mode's dirty little secret"

"It was different limos, different hotel floors. I don't think anyone spoke to Dave the entire tour."

MILLER

> **"I had to lay on the floor, just saying 'Yes or 'No'. At some point, I tried to get up and went into convulsions due to alcohol and drug withdrawal."**
>
> **GORE**

he reflects, twenty-five years on. "I could quite easily have punched his [Martin's] fucking lights out."

With Gahan's habit notably worsening and the singer more and more adrift from reality, the rest of the band attempted an intervention. It was not a success.

"They were genuinely concerned about my health, but of course I couldn't see that," Gahan later admitted to Q. "I said to Mart, 'Fuck off! Get off my back! You drink 15 pints of beer a night and take your clothes off and cause a scene! How can you be so hypocritical?'"

Gahan had a point. Gore was indeed drinking heroic amounts of lager per night, on one occasion informing his bandmates that he had drunk sixty-seven pints in eleven hours. It was a window into his nature that, amongst the carnage, he had taken the trouble to keep count.

By the time the European leg of the tour ended, on July 31, with a gig at Crystal Palace sports stadium

in south London in front of thirty-five thousand people, Gahan was entirely estranged from his three bandmates. By now, behind his back, they had a charming new nickname for him: "The Cunt."

Support at this show came from arch goth band the Sisters of Mercy. As he left the stage, their singer Andrew Eldritch made a sneering reference to Depeche Mode's onstage setup and Gahan's apparent relationship to his up-high bandmates: "Enjoy the puppet show!"

After Crystal Palace, Gore and Fletcher took downtime while Wilder flew to Dublin to mix a live *Songs of Faith and Devotion* album from tour recordings. Gahan partied on in Los Angeles. Reunited in the fall to take *Devotional* across North America, the band carried on falling apart at the seams.

The dates got off to an inauspicious start when Gahan and co-tour manager Daryl Bamonte, brother of Perry, were arrested and taken to a police station after the first show, in Quebec City, Canada, after Gahan punched a hotel security guard. Far, far worse was to come.

With Gahan increasingly strung out, it was becoming clear that his body could only cope with so much. At the show at Lakefront Arena in New Orleans on October 8, the skeletal singer collapsed as soon as he had left the stage as the set ended.

As frantic paramedics tended to Gahan backstage, his bandmates encored without him, playing an (unwittingly ironic) version of their movie soundtrack song, "Death's Door." In hospital, Gahan was told he had suffered a drug-induced heart attack.

"I was told by the doctor that I should continue the rest of the tour on a stool, because my heart probably wouldn't be able to take it," he later divulged. "I said, 'I can't do that!' So, we cancelled the next show—I got one day off—and then I just carried on."

In Los Angeles six weeks later, where the band were doing five sold-out nights at the seventeen-thousand-capacity Forum, Martin Gore's own partying led to him having a seizure during a meeting at the Sunset Marquis.

"I went to a club, met some guy who gave me some stuff, and was up all night until 9 or 10 in the morning," he later confessed. "We had a band meeting at 12 'o' clock and I managed to sleep for an hour.

"I got up and I've never felt so dreadful in my life. I managed literally to crawl to the meeting. I had to lay on the floor, just saying 'Yes' or 'No.' At some point, I tried to get up and went into convulsions due to alcohol and drug withdrawal."

"We were all sitting around this boardroom table, when Mart stood up and then went weird," confirmed Wilder. "He shook a bit, his eyes glazed over, and then he was on the floor convulsing."

After L.A., Depeche had two dates in Mexico City followed by a series of UK gigs culminating with a show at Wembley before Christmas. Few bands had ever been in more dire need of time off and apart—which didn't stop them making the worst decision imaginable.

The costs of the stage production and their expensive habits of top-of-the-range hotels and private jets meant that, despite selling close on a million tickets, Depeche had not yet made that much profit from *Devotional*. The idea arose that they should extend the tour.

It was a contentious topic. Gahan, Gore, and Wilder were eager to keep the party rolling and make more money. Frightened by his best friend Gore's collapse and at the end of his tether, Fletcher was dead against it. Daniel Miller also felt it was a terrible idea.

"I'd gone along to quite a number of dates and you couldn't talk to Dave because he was locked in

LEFT "Who's pulling your strings?" Andrew Eldritch, Sisters Of Mercy

RIGHT "I've never felt so dreadful in my life" - Martin Gore his dressing room," he recalled in *Depeche Mode: A Biography*. "Martin was drinking a lot and not enjoying it at all. Fletch was very tense and Al was very distant.

"Then this idea of going back to America came up. I personally was very against it and very vocal about it . . . if they wanted to make a lot of money out of it and that was the sole purpose of it, so be it. But they came out of it completely shot to pieces."

With a second wave of US arenas now scheduled for the spring, the band played ten dates in South Africa in February 1994. Alan Wilder was the next Depeche member to keel over, hospitalized for two days with alcohol-induced kidney stones.

Dismayed at the prospect of the extra dates, and of missing the birth of his second child, Fletcher sank deep into depression as the tour limped through Australia and Asia. His morose mood disturbed the partying Gahan and Wilder, who told Gore that they could not bear having him around.

"It was very difficult," Gore told *Q*, years later. "Andy has been my closest friend since we were 12. But for the other two, he'd become unbearable. I justified it by thinking that it would be better for Andy if he went home and got professional advice."

Fletcher was simply not up to the extra US leg and he wasn't going to try to be. After the Honolulu, Hawaii date on March 26, 1994, he quit the tour, flew to London, and checked back into the Priory. "I just lost it," he later admitted. "It was a breakdown." As a parting shot, he told Daniel Miller that he would never do another Mode tour while Wilder was in the band.

Daryl Bamonte, Wilder's main on-the-road partying buddy, took over Fletcher's keyboard parts as the tour lurched through South America in April. While in Chile, Dave Gahan heard that Nirvana singer Kurt Cobain had committed suicide.

"My first reaction was that I was angry," a shame-faced Gahan was to confess, years later. "I was pissed off. I felt like he had stolen my idea; he'd beaten me to it. That's how fucked-up I was. I really was that gone."

Like moths to a flame, the battered Mode returned to the US with a stripped-down, less costly version of *Devotional* for one for the road: a final string of thirty-four arena and auditorium dates. Martin Gore was to call them "the straw that broke the camel's back."

For these shows, the band made the seemingly suicidal decision to be supported by Primal Scream, then the most visibly chemically driven band in Britain. Gahan was the driving force behind this move.

"I'd picked the Scream because I'd heard that they liked to party," he said. "I really liked their record [*Screamadelica*] and it sounded like we'd be a good combination."

"Dave thought it would be great to have someone in a similar condition to him on the road," Wilder wryly confirmed. "He literally spent more time with them than with us. He would go and stand on the side of the stage and watch them play every night."

Gahan got into the habit of all-night jamming and partying sessions with the new arrivals. Primal Scream's antics included onstage fights and arrests for public nudity and drunkenness. In New York on June 16, *Select* journalist Andrew Perry joined the circus.

At a pre-show backstage gathering, Gahan was "shovelling cocaine up his nose at an alarming rate" when he beckoned Perry over. After talking to him briefly, he yelled at the writer that he would "curse him," bit him on the neck, and stormed out of the room.

"I assumed he was completely out of it," Perry, not unreasonably, later told *Q*. "But then, on stage, he was together and professional."

"I don't remember doing that," said Gahan, many years on. "I had some strange fascination at the time with vampires. I was starting to move into this place where I really believed what I was creating. I definitely could have been a vampire, in my own head. Even the bed that I slept in in Los Angeles was in the shape of a coffin—a huge double bed in the shape of a coffin."

After fourteen months and 156 shows, Depeche Mode's *Devotional* tour sputtered to a halt in fitting style in Indianapolis at the Deer Creek Music Center on July 8, 1994. Trying to leap into the crowd at the end of the show, Dave Gahan crashed shoulder-first into seats and a concrete floor, and was carted off to hospital.

"My body was going on nothing," he later reflected. "I cracked two ribs but it took me 24 hours to feel anything because I was so drunk. The next day I was in incredible pain. I was strapped up for three weeks."

Any sentient being observing Depeche Mode, and Dave Gahan in particular, at the end of the infernal *Devotional* tour would have imagined that the only way was up. They could not have been more wrong.

"Dave thought it would be great to have someone in a similar condition to him on the road. He literally spent more time with them than with us."

WILDER

Primal Scream: just what the doctor didn't order

9

ULTRA-DESTRUCTION

When the careering *Devotional* odyssey finally came to an end in summer 1994, three quarters of Depeche Mode began to rediscover some semblance of normality. Having missed the last few weeks of the jaunt, Andy Fletcher was out of rehab and doing well in his fight against depression.

Martin Gore slowed down his drinking, decompressed from the tour, and, on August 27, married his partner, Suzanne Boisvert, at a lavish ceremony in Hertfordshire. Dave Gahan arrived at the reception in the early hours with his new best friends, Primal Scream, with whom he had just jammed onstage at the Reading Festival.

Having begun a relationship with Miranda Sex Garden's Hepzibah Sessa on the road, Alan Wilder left his wife, Jeri, for the violinist. Just four days after Gore's wedding, the pair survived a near-death experience.

On a driving holiday in the Scottish Highlands, Wilder and Sessa were forced to swerve off the road when an RAF Tornado plane crashed into a hillside in Perthshire in front of their convertible. The two airmen on the plane were killed instantly. Wilder was to detail the incident in a press statement printed by *Melody Maker*:

> As I approached a sharp bend in the road, the sound of the Tornado appeared behind me, and as I looked up, I saw the underside of the aircraft no more than 50 feet above me. Within a split second, to my complete astonishment, the plane had crashed beside the road into the glen about 200 yards ahead. Apparently, it had been travelling at nearly 400 mph.
>
> As I swerved off the road into a farm track, I heard the sound of the impact and witnessed an enormous explosion from which the smoke and debris almost engulfed me.
>
> Another witness ran to call the police as I drove around the bend to the site. At the same time, particles of carbon, etc, began to rain down onto the open-top car.
>
> Beyond the bend, parts of the dead airmen's bodies were clearly visible in the road—parts of a seatbelt with guts attached, lumps of

gore, etc.; a parachute, burning shrapnel and a strong, sweet smell of fuel.

> After the police arrived, I decided to leave the scene . . . it was only at this point that I realised what an incredible escape I'd had. I would surely have been killed or, worse, severely maimed, had I been 10 seconds further into my journey.

Wilder was a blameless observer of this fatal incident—but another Depeche Mode member was rapidly, willfully upping the ante in his own cavalier dance with death.

Post-*Devotional* tour, Dave Gahan and his wife Teresa initially spent a few months partying hard in London: he has since identified this as the crucial juncture when his heroin habit got "completely out of hand." Yet he at least had enough insight to realize an unexpected suggestion by Conroy was hopelessly misguided.

"Teresa decided that she wanted to have a baby," he remembered, years later. "I said to her, 'Teresa—we're junkies.' When you're a junkie, you can't piss, shit, come . . . nothing. Those bodily functions go. You're in this soulless body. You're in a shell.

"The bottom line is, I didn't want to get clean. I thought I could control it. I thought I could maybe do it now and again, have a little party—little parties that lasted a month."

In the autumn of 1994, Gahan and Conroy returned to their home in Los Angeles, where the increasingly reclusive singer slipped deeper into addiction. In

"The bottom line is, I didn't want to get clean. I thought I could control it. I thought I could maybe do it now and again."

GAHAN

PREVIOUS PAGE Depeche Mode at the Meadows Amphitheter, Irvine, California

LEFT Dave Gahan's heroin habit "got completely out of hand"

> # "I was more worried about killing myself in a car accident, but I was quite happy to shoot dope in my arms. And over the years I was using daily."
>
> GAHAN

the textbook progression, heroin was no longer something that Dave Gahan did—it became his sole fixation, his entire *raison d'être*, as he was later to confess to *NME*:

> Wherever I was, I'd be thinking about it. And that's when you've got a problem. I'd wake up and think about it. I was a junkie with money—an endless supply of it!
>
> All I really wanted was my dope. I wasn't interested in cars or airplanes or all the other trappings of the rock star. I wasn't capable! I wouldn't dare get on my Harley because I was living up in the Canyons . . .
>
> That's the insanity of it. I was more worried about killing myself in a car accident, but I was quite happy to shoot dope in my arms. And over the years I was using daily.

Gahan fell into the same deadly routine as the one enacted by Kurt Cobain in his pre-suicide months of addiction, and the one brilliantly described by Mötley Crüe bassist Nikki Sixx in the addiction memoir that I co-wrote with him, *The Heroin Diaries*. He retreated to a closet in his apartment. It was his private space; his using space.

"I remember Kurt saying the same thing—he had a closet under the stairs," said Gahan. "That was plenty enough room. I was in there with my candle and my spoon, and that was it."

As his mental and physical health declined, the isolated Gahan was soon venturing out of his house only to score. As he was later to tell *Q* magazine, these missions soon acquired a nightmare quality.

"I was so fucking paranoid, I carried a .38 around with me at all times," he confessed. "Going downtown to cop, those guys you hang out with, they're heavy people. They have guns sitting on the table in front of them.

"I was scared of everything and everyone. I'd wait until four in the morning to check the mailbox and then walk down to the gate with the gun tucked in the back of my pants. I thought they were coming to get me—whoever 'they' were."

On Gahan's increasingly few social excursions, the people that he encountered were shocked by his wasted, dissipated appearance. Anton Corbijn got a phone call from another of his photo subjects, R.E.M.'s Michael Stipe: "He just said, 'I've seen Dave. I think you should give him a call.'"

A loving father, Gahan had previously always been able to keep it together when his son, Jack, came to stay with him, but soon even this was beyond him. Knowing he was in no state to cope with a visit in late 1994, he asked his mum to fly out to help him, as he later told *Q*:

> One night after I'd put Jack to bed and my mum was asleep, I got my outfit together and banged up in the living room. Then I blacked out; overdosed. When I woke up, I was sprawled across the bed. It was daylight and I heard voices from the kitchen. I thought, "Shit, I left all my shit out!"
>
> I got up in a panic, ran down to the living room and it was all gone. So I ran into the kitchen and Mum and Jack were sitting there, and I said, "What did you do with all my stuff, Mum?" She said, "I threw it in the rubbish outside."
>
> I ran outside and brought in six black bags, five of which were my neighbours, and emptied them out on the kitchen floor. I was on my hands and knees going through other people's garbage until I found what I needed. Then I shut myself in the bathroom.
>
> Shortly after that there's a knocking on the door. It bursts open and my son and my mother are there and I'm lying on the floor with the wounds open and everything. I say,

"All I really wanted was my dope"

"It's not what it looks like, Mum. I'm sick. I have to take steroids for my voice . . ." All this fucking trash comes out of my mouth.

Then I look up at my mum and she looks at me and I say, "Mum, I'm a junkie. I'm a heroin addict." And she says, "I know, love."

This wretched episode ended with Gahan's son taking his dad by the hand and urging him to see a doctor and "not be sick any more." His mother, returning to England days later, told him, "We don't want you to die." "Even that didn't stop me," Gahan was to admit. "That didn't do it."

The singer went into rehab in Arizona over Christmas 1994, and was to spend the first half of the following year in and out of such institutions. The lure of the needle, though, was way stronger than his wish to overcome it.

"I'd go to these meetings and be as fucking high as a kite among all these sober people," he later recalled. "I used to go to the bathroom and shoot up, then come back and raise my hand and say, 'I got 30 seconds clean!' I was taking the piss—but I was doing it to myself."

When Gahan did manage to buckle down in one six-week session in Arizona, he came out and told his wife that he felt he was on the mend. Her response was far from encouraging.

"We went to get some lunch and she said, 'I'm not going to stop drinking or taking drugs just because you have to,'" he explained. "She didn't use like me, regularly, but in rehab they said that if one of us wasn't going to give up, it would be impossible for the other.

"At that point I knew our relationship would have to be over if I was going to have any chance. I'd thought we loved each other. Now, I think the love was pretty one-sided."

Inevitably, Gahan began using again. Not long afterwards, his wife walked out on him. This separation was to trigger yet another bout of intense narcotic abuse.

"Trust issues have been going on all my life, so when Teresa left I was then given the excuse to go out and get even more fucked up," he said. "I was hell-bent on going the whole hog. My wife had left me, my friends were disappearing so I was surrounded by a bunch of junkies.

"I knew exactly what was going on. I had money, I had drugs and that was why they were around me. It fuelled my anger even more."

Gahan's spiral of decline increased inexorably. On one occasion, he woke up on a Hollywood dealer's lawn, having OD'd in the house. The dealer had stolen his wallet, watch, and jewelry and chucked him on the lawn for dead. Having come to, the singer banged on the door. The woman who opened it was wearing his watch.

A few days later, Gahan was back at the same house to buy more drugs. "I had to," he later reasoned to Q. "They were my so-called friends."

As Gahan perfected the art of falling apart on one side of the Atlantic there was a major development for Depeche Mode on the other. Alan Wilder announced

that he was leaving the band. He had not made the decision lightly. Wilder had become more and more frustrated by what he perceived as the uneven workload in the band and a lack of appreciation, particularly from Gore, of his many hours in the studio. He had also come to resent being paid the same for his efforts as Fletcher, who remained resolutely non-musical.

Wilder called a meeting with Gore and Fletcher in London to inform them of his decision. Their reactions were arguably yet more proof that human interaction has never exactly been Depeche Mode's strong suit.

"Martin was fine but Fletch seemed to take it quite personally, which I couldn't really understand," he told Steve Malins in *Depeche Mode: A Biography*.

"I said to him, 'Look, I've just had enough of being in a group. I'm not particularly enjoying it.' He seemed to take it as a personal affront, somehow. Martin didn't. He just said, 'Yeah, OK,' and shook my hand."

With Gahan, the member he had been closest to, AWOL and failing to respond to phone calls, Wilder

was left with no choice in those pre-email days but to fax the singer the news of his departure: "I sent him a fax saying, 'Look, I've tried to call you, Dave. I can't get hold of you. I've just had a meeting with the others to say I've left the group. Good luck.'" He again heard nothing back.

Wilder did, however, issue a press statement on his exit, on his thirty-sixth birthday on August 1, 1995, that confirmed that the split was a long way from being amicable—on his part, at least:

> Due to increasing dissatisfaction with the internal relations and working practices of the group, it is with some sadness that I have decided to part company from Depeche Mode. My decision to leave the group was not an easy one, particularly as the last few albums were an indication of the full potential that Depeche Mode were realising.
>
> Since joining in 1982, I have continually striven to give total energy, enthusiasm and commitment to the furthering of the group's success and, in spite of a consistent imbalance in the distribution of the workload, willingly offered this. Unfortunately, within the group, this level of input never received the respect and acknowledgment that it warrants.
>
> Whilst I believe that the calibre of our musical output has improved, the quality of our association has deteriorated to the point where I no longer feel that the end justifies the means. I have no wish to cast aspersions on any individual: suffice to say that relations have become seriously strained, increasingly frustrating and ultimately, in certain situations, intolerable. Given these circumstances, I have no option but to leave the group . . .

It was a pretty damning kiss-off—yet was Wilder right to feel that he had been routinely undervalued by his bandmates? Daniel Miller, for one, felt that he was probably justified in feeling aggrieved.

"I've always thought he was underrated by the others," he reflected in *Depeche Mode: A Biography*. "Or rather, Dave valued what he did. Fletch played down what he did and Martin was just off in his world and didn't really think about it.

Alan Wilder: "I have no option but to leave the group"

"Suffice to say that relations have become seriously strained, increasingly frustrating and ultimately, in certain situations, intolerable."

WILDER

"It wasn't just the musical element. Alan was the one who took the trouble to check things and listen to the cuts. He looked at the artwork, and so on. He took a lot of interest in all the aspects of it."

Depeche Mode were a man down—and there was no guarantee that it would stop there. In California, Dave Gahan's precipitous decline was about to hit crisis point, and to become very public.

On August 9, 1995, Gahan checked out of his second stint in rehab clinic in Arizona. Unable to face his empty Hollywood Hills home, with Conroy now gone, he checked into his regular party haunt of the Sunset Marquis, just off Sunset Boulevard.

Just over a week later, on August 17, he called at his house to collect some clothes. The place had been comprehensively ransacked. His two Harley Davidson bikes, home studio, hi-fi, and furniture had all been taken, as had tapes of songs he'd been working on.

The burglars had clearly known his home security code—and, to add insult to injury, had even reset it with a new code when they left. It made Gahan realize that the thieves were people he knew.

"It must have been an inside job," he was to reflect. "Some of my so-called friends had gone in there, knowing I was in rehab. I thought, 'I can't believe this—this is my fucking life!' My little world, Daveworld, was falling apart."

"Hellbent on destruction," Gahan returned to the Sunset Marquis, where a female friend came over to see him. What happened next he later related to *Q* magazine:

I quickly got loaded and drank a lot of wine, and took a handful of pills. I rang my mother and she said Teresa had told her that I hadn't been to any rehab and wasn't even trying to get clean, like I had promised. But I was trying: I was doing the best I could.

I was in the middle of that phone call to my mum and I told her to hold on, I'd be back in a minute. I went to the bathroom and cut my wrists with a razor, wrapped towels around them and came back to the phone. I said, "Mum, I've got to go, I love you very much."

Then I sat down with my friend and acted like nothing was going on. I put my arms down by my side and I could feel them bleeding away. I had cut deep, so I couldn't even feel my fingers any more. My friend didn't have a clue what was happening until she noticed a pool of blood gathering on the floor.

Gahan slumped into unconsciousness as his panicking friend dialled 911. L.A.'s paramedics were by now no strangers to his address: only later did Gahan learn they had nicknamed him "The Cat" because of the number of lives he had used up.

With blood pouring out and no time to administer an anesthetic, the paramedics stitched up Gahan's wrists without one. One of them also found time to ring a radio DJ, Richard Blade on KROQ, and tell him what had happened. On the air, Blade announced: "I think Dave Gahan has tried to commit suicide."

The singer came to in Cedars-Sinai Medical Center, in a straitjacket: "I was in a psychiatric ward, a padded room. For a minute, I thought I might be in Heaven, whatever Heaven is. Then this psychiatrist informed me that I'd committed a crime under local law by trying to take my own life. Only in fucking L.A., huh?"

Back in London, Depeche Mode's Mute Records PR, Mick Paterson, was by now used to fielding media enquiries about Dave Gahan's health. "I'd lie," he admits now. "I'd give them something, but it wouldn't be the real story. You just make something up.

"The funny thing was that Erasure were much bigger in the UK than Depeche then. Their singer, Andy Bell, was a real character who liked a night out, so I used to get more calls from the tabloids about Andy than about Dave."

Mute put out a brief, factual statement: "Dave Gahan, lead singer of Depeche Mode, was admitted to Cedars-Sinai Medical Center in Beverly Hills, California, yesterday morning. He is resting comfortably and expects to be released soon." It was no use. The Cat was out of the bag. Three days later, a UK tabloid, the *Daily Mirror*, ran a story with a typically lurid headline:

ROCK STAR "DEATH BID"

Discharged from Cedars-Sinai after a few days' recuperation, with no police charges, Gahan went back to the Sunset Marquis and carried on where he had left off. If his suicide attempt had been a wake-up call, he certainly was not heeding it.

"As soon as I'd got out, I was up to my old tricks," he later revealed. "I'd clean up a bit, then use again, and every time I needed more, I wanted it quicker. There was never enough: I just had to keep fucking going until I blacked out, or whatever.

"That's my problem. Any addict's problem. They don't know when to stop. I didn't know when to stop. I went from worse to worse."

It was by now more than a year since Depeche Mode had finished up the sprawling *Devotional* tour and, suitably refreshed and recovered, Martin Gore and Andrew Fletcher were ready to get things moving again. The question was: was there a band still there to move?

With Alan Wilder departed, and Dave Gahan apparently on the verge of departing the world, Depeche looked in a truly parlous state. Was it worth getting back in the studio for a group who seemed no longer to be a going concern?

Daniel Miller offered them a useful halfway house. Minded to put out a new greatest hits album to follow up *The Singles 81—85*, he suggested to Gore that he first wrote two new songs to go on there. He also had an innovative idea for their producer.

Inspired by an offhand Gore comment that he would prefer the new material to sound "quite hip-hop," Miller suggested that they look to Tim Simenon, who had enjoyed considerable British chart success with his electronic music project, Bomb the Bass.

As a producer, Simenon had helped to shape major hits for Neneh Cherry and Adamski and worked with John Foxx. Crucially, he was also a big Depeche fan who had previously remixed "Everything Counts" and "Enjoy The Silence," among others.

Simenon was quickly on board, and in October 1995 the troubled Gahan flew over to join Gore and Fletcher for exploratory recording sessions. Yet the

ailing singer was far from sure that Depeche Mode had a future, given both his own condition and the loss of Wilder.

"To be honest, I felt that if anything was going to split up the band, that [Wilder quitting] was what it was," he later admitted. "A very valuable person had left. Suddenly, musically, for me, there was a big hole. That inspiration and musicality wasn't there."

Nevertheless, when the band convened with Simenon at Eastcote Studio, near to Mute in west London, Gahan liked the early demos that Gore played to them enough to get fired up again.

"I really wanted to record them," he was to say. "I really wanted to do the songs. A lot of the lyrical content and the feeling in the melodies really fitted with the way I was feeling and the stuff I was going through.

"It seemed like it would be a really good thing for me to do at that time because it was a way for me to work through my own personal problems. In retrospect, I wasn't ready and it was more important for me to take heroin than being in the band."

> **"I went to the bathroom and cut my wrists with a razor, wrapped towels around them and came back to the phone. I said, 'Mum, I've got to go, I love you very much.'"**
>
> **GAHAN**

"Quite hip-hop?" Send for Tim Simenon

Over six weeks in London, they worked on three Gore compositions: "Sister of Night," "Useless," and "Insight." Gahan's habit and unstable mental state and Fletcher's lack of musical suss made them irregular presences in the studio, but Gore and the similarly quiet, low-key Simenon soon bonded over the studio console.

"I hardly ever saw Dave Gahan in the studio and Fletch would drop by, but Martin and I put a lot of hours in," Simenon told Steve Malins in *Depeche Mode: A Biography*. "There were fun times but generally it was fucking hard work. Martin and I did a lot of chin-scratching.

"Martin doesn't discuss the music a lot of the time. I'd try to get him to talk about it, but generally if it's right he won't say anything. If it isn't, he will, and then he'll suggest another idea."

The sessions were promising enough for Depeche to resolve to make another album and a second Eastcote session later that year yielded more tracks including the terse, attitudinal "Barrel of a Gun." Tired of flying to London, Gahan insisted that the third studio encounter, in April 1996, should be in New York.

It was not a success. Arriving at the Jimi Hendrix-founded Electric Lady Studios in Greenwich Village, Simenon, Gore, and Fletcher quickly realized that Gahan's habit had, if anything, worsened. Wasted and exhausted, the singer was simply incapable of performing.

"He was hiding his habit from us again—lying to us," Gore was to summarize. "He was saying things like, 'Alice In Chains are in town next week but they won't want to hang around with me any more now that I'm clean!'"

"Ninety per cent of the time I was still strung out, and the rest of the time I was sick from kicking," Gahan later admitted. "It became very obvious that, physically, I couldn't stand up in front of a microphone for more than an hour without wanting to lay down and die."

The sessions yielded only one Gahan vocal, for "Sister of Night," and even that was pieced together by Simenon from numerous aborted takes. Remarkably, Gahan now claims it is one of his favorite Mode vocal performances: "I can hear how scared I was. I'm glad it's there to remind me. I could see the pain I was causing everybody."

Writing off the New York fiasco as a bad job, the band asked Gahan to focus on getting better in L.A. The singer agreed to see a singing coach, Evelyn Halus, after which Tim Simenon would fly out to record Gahan's vocals in a Hollywood studio near his home.

Gahan paid lip service to the plan, but that was all it was. By now he was dating an actress, Jennifer Sklias, whom he had met in rehab in Arizona. As he bade her farewell in New York, she knew what was on his mind.

"As I left, she looked me in the eye and said, 'You're going to get high,'" he was to relate. "I said, 'Yep.' She said, 'You don't have to.' I said, 'I do.' And I went home and had the worst binge I'd ever had."

By now renting an apartment in Santa Monica, Gahan chose instead to head back to the scene of his worst excesses, the Sunset Marquis. Once checked in on the evening of May 27, 1996, he headed for oblivion one more time—or, maybe, one last time.

Having met a girl in the hotel bar, Gahan took her up to his room and called a dealer, who came over. By now, with heroin alone having an increasingly weak effect on him, he was in the habit of injecting coke and heroin speedballs, which he now proceeded to do.

"It was a particularly strong brand of heroin called 'Red Rum,' which has killed quite a few people," he later told *Q* magazine. "Of course, I just thought it referred to the racehorse, until someone pointed out that it spells 'murder' backwards."

At 1am on May 28, as the girl waited in his bedroom, Gahan watched the dealer fill the syringe for him in the bathroom.

"There was something weird about that night," he was to tell Q. "I remember saying to the guy, 'Don't fill the rig up. Don't put too much coke in.' I felt wrong."

It seems the dealer did not listen. Minutes after injecting, Gahan OD'd in the bathroom. Having dragged the comatose singer into the bedroom, the panicking dealer ran off, briefly returning a couple of minutes later to collect his gear and his needles.

Left alone with the apparently lifeless Gahan, the terrified woman dialled 911. As she awaited the paramedics, she tried to bring him around by throwing water on him. It didn't work. Gahan went into cardiac arrest and began to turn blue.

When the medics arrived to tend to the Cat one last time, he looked a hopeless cause. Fibrillating him in the ambulance as it raced, once again, to Cedars-Sinai, they miraculously managed to kick-start his heart. Somehow, he was still alive. But as Gahan later told *NME*:

All I remember about it was it was really black and really scary, and I remember feeling that it was wrong. This was something really not supposed to be happening.

I woke up in hospital hearing one of the paramedics saying, "I think we lost him." I sat up and said, "No you fucking haven't!" But I'd had the full cardiac arrest. My heart had stopped for two minutes. I'd been dead, basically.

A detective read me my rights and I was arrested for possession of cocaine and needles. I was handcuffed to a trolley. Straight from hospital, they threw me into the county jail for a couple of nights in a cell with about seven other guys.

It was a scary experience—but not enough to scare me into quitting.

Jonathan Kessler paid Gahan's $10,000 bail money to spring him from the L.A. County Sheriff's Office. With Gore, Fletcher, and Daniel Miller five thousand miles away in London, Kessler was routinely the only Depeche camp man that Gahan had to turn to in a crisis. By now the band's manager, he had often filled that role without complaint.

However, Kessler was unable to deter the impulsive Gahan from giving the media and paparazzi gathered outside the Sheriff's Office a spontaneous if somewhat incoherent lowdown on his condition. As the flash bulbs popped, he began:

> I'm a heroin addict. I've been fighting to get off heroin for a year. I've been in rehab twice and I don't want to be like people like Kurt, and stuff like that. I want to be a survivor.
>
> I mean, I died again last night. So, I'm not . . .

"This was something really not supposed to be happening"

I'm not . . . my Cat's lives are out. I just want to say sorry to all the fans and stuff, and I'm glad to be alive, and sorry to my mum as well.

I just want them to know that it's not cool. It's not a cool thing to be an addict. You're a slave to it, and it's taken everything away from me that I loved, and so I'm going to rebuild my life.

Gahan may have sincerely believed the words when he said them but they did not translate into action. Using junkie logic, he told Kessler his OD had only happened because the dealer sold him dodgy gear. Returning to the Sunset Marquis, he carried on shooting up for two or three days.

"Then I went back to the house I'd rented in Santa Monica and sat on the couch and realised I was going nowhere," he was to relate. "I thought I was going to die. When I shot up, there was absolutely no feeling at all."

Gahan phoned his girlfriend, Jennifer Sklias, herself a recovering addict, in New York, but she was unable to help. By now, he knew that he wanted to stop: he just didn't know how to do it. Luckily for him, the decision was about to be taken out of his hands.

Jonathan Kessler phoned Gahan and asked him to come to a legal meeting about his arrest. The singer arrived to find this story was a smokescreen. The Depeche Mode manager was instead staging a full-on intervention.

Kessler had called in Bob Timmins, a Los Angeles drugs counsellor who specialized in helping celebrities and public figures to overcome their addiction. A former addict who had spent years in jail, including for armed robbery, his previous rock-star client list included members of the Rolling Stones, Aerosmith, Mötley Crüe, and Red Hot Chili Peppers.

Kessler and Timmins informed Gahan that he was going back into rehab—now.

"I said, 'No fucking way,'" Gahan was to admit. "They said, 'You are.' I said, 'All right, tomorrow'—thinking I could go home and cook up before I went. They said, 'No, now.' I was like, 'What about this evening?' 'No.'

"I said, 'A couple of hours, I need to call my mum.' They let me go. Jonathan said he'd come and pick me up. I went home, did my last deal, had my last little party and checked into the rehab."

"I was sick of hurting everyone around me. I didn't want to lose my son. I didn't want him to grow up wondering why his dad killed himself."

GAHAN

Gahan and attorney in court after his overdose

Compared to his previous, fairly relaxed rehab experiences, Exodus Recovery in Marina del Rey operated a hard-line regime. The jail-like routine began with 7am daily meetings, with residents initially not allowed to leave the complex. Gahan's fellow patients included the Hollywood actor Robert Downey Jr.

It worked. Over the excruciating first couple of weeks, Gahan went cold turkey and detoxed. At times he was strapped down while his battered, beaten body underwent withdrawal seizures. It was a grim, painful process—but he saw it through.

Gahan's progress in rehab led the Californian justice system to be lenient with him when he appeared in court on July 30, dropping all charges as long as he remained clean. He would have to take urine tests every fortnight. Any lapse would mean a swift return to jail.

This draconian deterrent was obviously a major reason why Dave Gahan, after five soul-destroying years, was finally clear of heroin. Yet just as significant was the fact that it was the outcome that he craved with every bruised fiber of his being.

"I was sick of hurting everybody around me," he told Q magazine. "I didn't want to lose my son. I didn't want him to grow up wondering why his dad killed himself. All of that hit harder and harder.

"And suddenly I got it. There was hope. I could change. I could have a choice . . . and now I have a choice every day. I have a choice about what I want to do, where I want to go, how I want to be."

Gahan realized that this second chance, this new life, would require total sobriety: if he drank again, drugs would surely follow. After four weeks in Exodus, he spent six months in a Los Angeles court-ordered "sober living house" with fellow addicts and finally recorded more vocals for the new Depeche Mode album with Tim Simenon in a local studio.

Evelyn Halus, the voice coach hired by Depeche to coax life back into Gahan's voice, was to prove an invaluable ally. She began taking the singer each Sunday morning to a church in a rough part of downtown L.A. to sing with the choir.

"She said, 'You come with me and sing with the whole group. You've got to be part of a team!' Gahan told loudandquiet.com. "She was so nice and gentle with me and gave me a lot of her time. She kind of brought my voice back to me."

Throughout Gahan's life-and-death crises, Simenon, Martin Gore, and Andy Fletcher had been continuing to work on the album, which was by now called Ultra, at Abbey Road studios in London. It was decided that Gahan would join them to wrap things up.

This band reunion could have been a painful and resentful process. In the end, it went just fine.

"In some ways, maybe it [Gahan's public meltdown] took a bit of pressure off us," the ever-understated Gore was to muse. "No-one expected an album at all, let alone a good one."

"Dave came good in the end," acknowledged Fletcher, simply. "He gave up drugs and drink and got all his vocals done. He got himself together, basically."

"I think the fact that they made that album was a shock to everybody who was close to the band," Daniel Miller was to admit. "And to the media, who were watching the band."

The remarkable thing was that Ultra wasn't just another Depeche Mode album—it was a great one. The tone was set by lead single "Barrel of a Gun," a UK No. 4, whose Anton Corbijn-filmed video saw Gahan, eyes closed, stumbling disorientated around Morocco with a gun trained on him.

Gahan, unsurprisingly, saw the promo as "quite autobiographical": "I wanted it to be like you're constantly running away from your life, avoiding life, avoiding your feelings . . . it's being a junkie, basically."

Compared to the relatively jamming-based, bluesy Songs of Faith and Devotion, Ultra was an undoubted return to Depeche's electronica motherlode, thanks to a large degree to producer Simenon. Where Alan Wilder was prone to sonic flourishes, Simenon kept it minimal—and real.

Probably Ultra's standout track was "It's No Good," put out in March 1997, two weeks before the album's release. Another UK top five hit, it benefited from another sharp Corbijn video, this time capturing Gahan throwing rock-star shapes in a dingy variety club.

Released on April 14, 1997, the album got Depeche's usual mixed bag of critical notices. Vox magazine sniffed, "The more you listen to this album, the worse it seems to get," while The Times detected a "weary" tone to the record: "It sounds as if, instead of providing inspiration, all the angst they have been through has simply worn them out."

However, more perceptive reviewers detected dark, buried treasures beneath the sleek, alluring surface hum. Writing in Q magazine, band supporter—and,

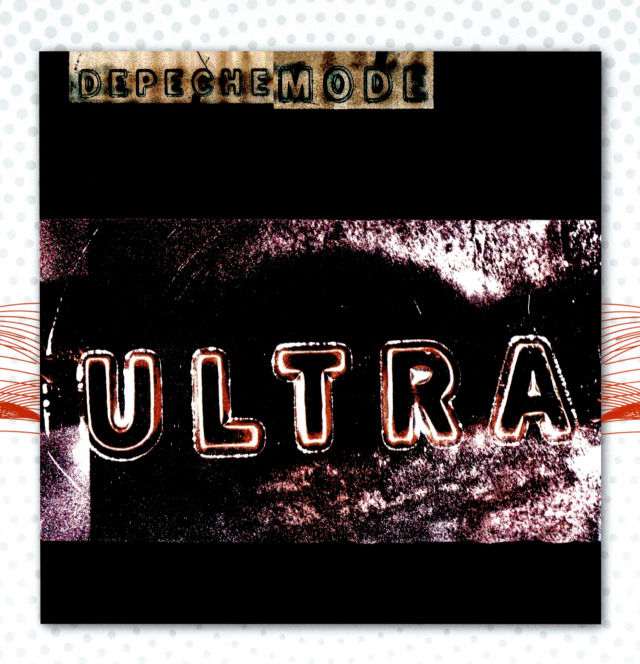

"It's an album of dry,
dislocated, burnt-out and sometimes
beautiful songwriting."

Q

Ultra

TRACK LIST

Barrel of A Gun

The Love Thieves

Home

It's No Good

Uselink

Useless

Sister of Night

Jazz Thieves

Freestate

The Bottom Line

Insight

Junior Painkiller

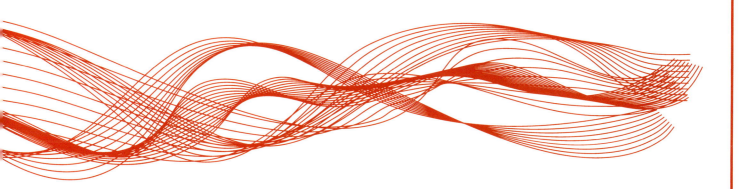

Recorded at Abbey Road, Eastcote, Westside, Strongroom, RAK Studios, London, England; Electric Lady, New York and Larrabee West, Los Angeles, USA

Produced by Tim Simenon & Depeche Mode

Personnel
Dave Gahan
Martin Gore
Andy Fletcher

Cover art
Anton Corbijn

Released 14 Apr 1997

Label Mute CD STUMM 148

Highest chart position on release
UK 1, GER 1, FRA 1, SWE 2, CAN 5, SWI 2, US 1, ITA 6, AUS 14, SPA 3

later, biographer—Steve Malins wrote: "It's an album of dry, dislocated, burnt-out and sometimes beautiful songwriting. It sounds lived-in and dirty, rather than a bit pervy and self-consciously bleak."

On the release of *Ultra*, the open book that is Dave Gahan gave a series of candid, confessional interviews about his addiction, suicide attempt, OD, and recovery. The journalists knew a good story when they heard one, and this narrative dominated media coverage of the record.

Gahan himself was to regret his honesty—"Even in ten years' time, all I'll be to the press is Dave the junkie!"—but his transparency about his plight and survival triggered empathy and love among the band's long-term fans. The most diehard flocked to two low-key *Ultra* release shows, in Adrenalin Village in London and the Shrine Exposition Hall in Los Angeles.

The band would not, however, tour the album. Dave Gahan was on the mend but nowhere near ready for that yet. "It's taken this long to find out what I really want to do with myself," he noted, "and it's certainly not to go out on tour." Martin Gore was equally frank: "We don't feel we can survive another tour."

Ultra, the album which looked for so long like it would either never exist or would serve as a posthumous tribute to Depeche Mode's singer, became the band's second UK No. 1, as well as topping the chart in Germany. In the US, it hit a respectable No. 5.

Depeche Mode, and Dave Gahan in particular, had been to hell and back and had somehow returned to tell the tale. They had survived the era of Ultra-destruction. But it had been a fucking close thing.

LEFT Depeche launch *Ultra* at the Shrine Auditorium in L.A.
RIGHT Fletcher and Gahan in Berlin: gold discs for *Ultra* all round

10

THE CALM AFTER THE STORM

Newly sober, Dave Gahan knew that he had to get away from Los Angeles, the city of his excesses that held so many grim memories for him. He had been granted a fresh start to his life and that was not the place to make it.

Luckily, Gahan was assured of welcoming arms and a cosy haven on the other coast of the US. His relationship with girlfriend, actress, and fellow recovering addict Jennifer Sklias was blossoming, and late in 1997 he moved to New York to be with her and her son, James.

It was an exciting time of new beginnings and Gahan had little reason to leave NY in early 1998. However, in the spring of that year he flew back to London to reconvene with Gore, Fletcher, and *Ultra* producer Tim Simenon to record a new Depeche Mode single.

The lush, textured "Only When I Lose Myself" was, said Gore, about the obsessional nature of love, and was Depeche Mode at their most reflective and elegiac. Released on September 7 as a harbinger of an imminent *The Singles 86>98* greatest hits album, it squeezed into the UK Top 20 (and made No. 1 in Spain).

On its release later that month, the compilation did remarkably well. It was a different, darker creature than 1985's perky, bright-eyed *The Singles 81–85* but an equally salutary reminder of what a great singles band Depeche could be. Top five in Britain, it unsurprisingly topped the chart in Germany.

The band also made a bold and, given their troubled times on the road in recent years, brave decision—they would tour the album.

The four-month jaunt at the end of 1998 was announced at a press conference in Cologne, which Martin Gore opened in impish mode: "I'm very sorry, Alan couldn't make it!" However, at least one band member viewed the prospect of weeks on tour with some trepidation.

Confessing that he was "scared" of returning to the environment where his drug habit had first taken root, Dave Gahan pounded the gym treadmill for six weeks before *The Singles Tour* kicked off. His bandmate Gore also resolved to drink only twice per week.

PREVIOUS PAGE Shoreline Amphitheater in Mountain View, California
LEFT *The Singles Tour* reaches Kölnarean, Cologne
RIGHT Happy days are here again

In the event, the tour ran remarkably smoothly. The stripped-down Anton Corbijn stage presentation put the spotlight firmly on Gahan, as the visual focus, and on the music. As the set comprised almost exclusively later-career hit singles, it was rapturously received.

Tim Simenon, who DJ'd as a tour support act, saw that Dave Gahan was being well protected from any potentially fatal lapse. "No drugs were allowed," he told Steve Malins in *Depeche Mode: A Biography*.

"That was completely stated to crew and band. I like vodka, but I wasn't allowed that in the dressing room. It was just literally beer and wine."

As it swung from first-ever visits to Estonia, Latvia, and Russia, where they were greeted like gods, through Europe and on to two months in America, the tour was nonetheless a happy place to be. Gore and Gahan both found a childlike wonder in actually going onstage sober.

"They were really able to appreciate the audiences and see what was going on a lot more than they ever did before," Daniel Miller was to observe. "They came back saying it was great and they were really feeding off each other on stage."

Joining the tour at Berlin's open-air Waldbühne amphitheater on September 18, a journalist from a UK Sunday newspaper, the *Observer*, marveled at the presence of "21,000 Euro-goths" before making a pertinent point about Depeche Mode's Gore-

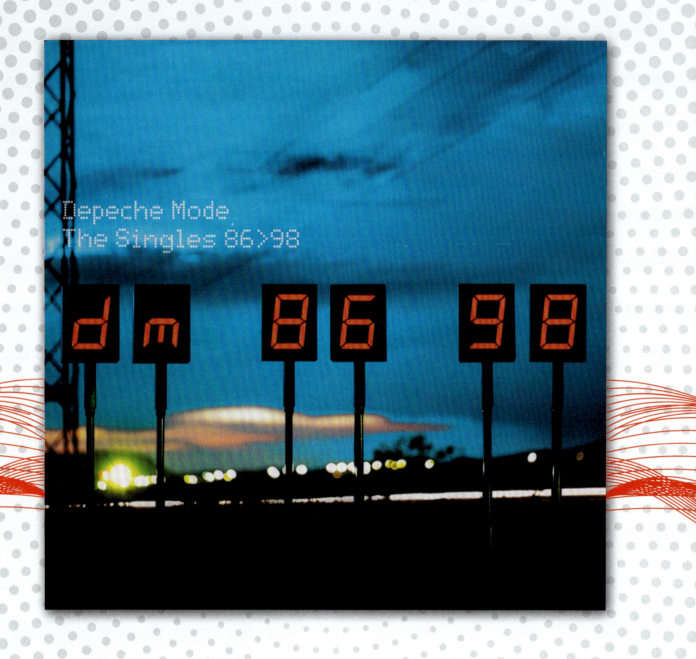

Depeche Mode
The Singles 86>98

dm 86 98

"A different, darker creature than 1985's perky, bright-eyed *The Singles 81–85* but an equally salutary reminder of what a great singles band Depeche could be."

Singles 86>98

TRACK LIST

Stripped

A Question of Lust

A Question of Time

Strangelove

Never Let Me Down Again

Behind the Wheel

Personal Jesus

Enjoy the Silence

Policy of Truth

World in My Eyes

I Feel You

Walking in My Shoes

Condemnation

In Your Room

Barrel of A Gun

It's No Good

Home

Useless

Only When I Lose Myself

Little 15

Everything Counts (Live)

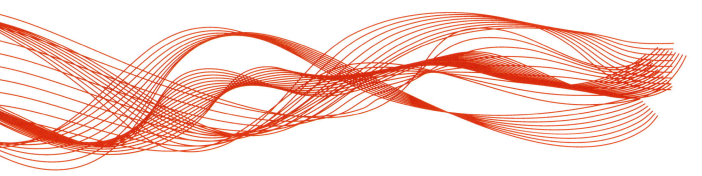

Produced by Dave Bascombe, Depeche Mode, Flood, Gareth Jones, Daniel Miller and Tim Simenon

Personnel
Dave Gahan
Martin Gore
Andy Fletcher
Alan Wilder

Cover art
Mat Cook

Released 28 Sept 1998

Label Mute CDMUTEL5

Highest chart position on release
UK 5, GER 1, FRA 6, SWE 1, SWI 3, AUS 42, CAN 14, ITA 2, SPA 8, US 38

Gahan axis: "On stage, it's clear how much they need each other. Gore alone is an anonymous wisp; Gahan alone a trite rock pastiche. Together, they are oddly convincing."

After the tour wrapped up in California just before Christmas, Dave Gahan stayed in America, where on Valentine's Day 1999 he married Jennifer Sklias after converting to Greek Orthodox Christianity. Four months later, the couple had a daughter, Stella Rose.

Meanwhile, in Hertfordshire, Martin Gore was attempting to begin writing the next Depeche Mode album—and not doing at all well.

Trying to write material in his home studio, Gore found that he was getting nowhere. Songs were begun and then abandoned as writer's block set in. Six months in, he decided to draft in some help.

Gore asked Gareth Jones, the engineer/producer whose association with Depeche went right back to *Construction Time Again*, and a programmer friend, Paul Freegard, to work with him. Their arrival in his home gave him the necessary jolt as he had to give them some songs to work with.

The trio worked up demos of five Gore songs before Depeche Mode turned their mind to the question of who should produce their next record. One particular studio man of the moment had caught Gore's attention.

Mark Bell was the co-founder of techno duo LFO, and in recent years had made a name in electronic music circles as the producer of two Björk divine divination albums, *Homogenic* and the *Dancer in the Dark* movie soundtrack, *Selmasongs*. Bell was delighted to receive an exploratory phone call from Daniel Miller.

"I had no time to think about it," Bell told Jonathan Miller in his book *Stripped*. "They just said, 'Right, do you want to start in a week?'

"Depeche Mode were really important to me when I was 15 or 16. I liked how they always treated electronics and acoustics as one entity. Their music doesn't belong to any particular genre. It's not clichéd in any way.

"So, when I got the chance to work with them I thought it would be really weird, but it didn't seem weird at all. I'd already done a remix of 'Home' from *Ultra* and they had really liked how I interpreted the song."

The millennium was to bring major life changes for Martin Gore as in spring 2000 he relocated with his family to Santa Barbara, California. Gahan, Fletcher,

Bell, and Jones joined him there in June to work on the album that was to become *Exciter*.

With all band members in uncharacteristically sunny, happy frames of mind, the record came together at a gentle pace. Compared to the frazzled tensions, abandoned sessions, and personal meltdowns of *Ultra*, the process was positively serene.

"It was quite relaxed most of the time," the newly chilled Gahan was to report. "We have our own routines and other things but it was pretty laid-back. It was a very positive experience."

Yet maybe it was rather too free of strife and tensions. When the completed *Exciter* appeared, on May 14, 2001, it sounded a little too much like Depeche Mode were firmly in their comfort zone: at times, on autopilot. It was not an album that merited its title.

Mark Bell's subtle, nuanced input ensured that sonically the album was never less than sumptuous and inviting, but too many of the tracks seemed to float by in a low-level, soporific hum. *Exciter* was notably one-paced and that pace was a mellow, ambient reverie.

Inevitably, there were standouts. "When the Body Speaks," recorded in one take with Gahan crooning over Gore's acoustic guitar before Bell laded electro-atmospherics on top, was a fragile delight, even if it hardly justified Gore's excitable description of it as "like the Righteous Brothers playing next to a rave."

An anomaly on the album, "The Dead of Night" found Gahan back in rock monster mode, drawling a louche number that Gore said was inspired by watching drug-taking in VIP London private members' clubs: "We're in the zombie room/Eating from silver spoons."

"I had a lot of fun on 'The Dead of Night,'" Gahan was to admit. "I got to be Gahan on that, big-time . . . play out all my fantasy Bowie-esque stuff, Iggy stuff, and [be] the dark, gothic man."

With attitude and a pulse, the song sounded like it belonged on a different Depeche Mode album than *Exciter*, with its procession of slight, wistful ambient pieces. Gahan sang the closing "Goodnight Lovers" as if crooning a lullaby to his new daughter, Stella Rose. It wasn't the only track on the record that sounded sleep-inducing.

The fault didn't lie with Bell's electro-alchemy or with Gahan, who was in fine, reborn voice. Rather, the suspicion hovered that when Martin Gore moved to California, he forgot to pack any songs.

Some reviewers were surprisingly positive about *Exciter*, welcoming the trio's clear newfound peace of mind. However, the *Los Angeles Times* astutely commented that some fans would "look nostalgically to the cheap thrills of the past when Depeche Mode were content to make disposable pop," and Gareth Grundy, in *Q* magazine, cut right to the heart of the problem.

"At best, *Exciter* is superficially attractive; an exercise in good taste that mixes contemporary droning with shuffling drums and guitar," he wrote. "It's pleasant enough wrapping that slips easily around Dave Gahan's recharged vocals.

"This time, it's Martin Gore who's out of puff. No amount of fashionable tweaking can hide the flimsiness of his offerings."

There was little prospect of *Exciter* repeating the UK chart-topping triumph of *Ultra*, and the album peaked at No. 9. However, it also went Top 10 in the US and hit No. 1 in a slew of European countries, including France and Germany.

"This time, it's Martin Gore who's out of puff. No amount of fashionable tweaking can hide the flimsiness of his offerings."

Q

Gahan and Gore at Wembley Arena

"At best, *Exciter* is superficially attractive; an exercise in good taste that mixes contemporary droning with shuffling drums and guitar."

Q

Exciter

TRACK LIST

Dream On

Shine

The Sweetest Condition

When the Body Speaks

The Dead of Night

Lovetheme

Freelove

Comatose

I Feel Loved

Breathe

Easy Tiger

I Am You

Goodnight Lovers

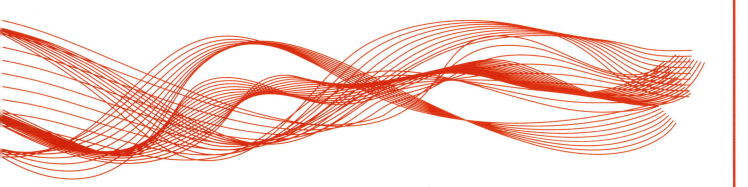

Recorded at RAK Studios, Sarm West Studios, London, England; Sound Design, Santa Barbara, Electric Lady Studios and Sony Music Studios, New York, USA

Produced by Mark Bell, Gareth Jones & Depeche Mode

Personnel
Dave Gahan
Martin Gore
Andy Fletcher

Cover art
Form

Released 14 May 2001

Label Mute CDSTUMM 190

Highest chart position on release
UK 9, GER 1, FRA 1, SWE 1, CAN 3, SWI 2, US 8, ITA 2, AUS 20, SPA 2

Contemplating the solo life

The subsequent six-month *Exciter* tour was also a success, reaching more than one-and-a-half-million fans in eighty-four arenas in twenty-four countries. On some European dates, support came from Frank Tovey, aka Fad Gadget, the Mute founding artist whom Depeche Mode had been supporting at the Canning Town Bridge House when Daniel Miller discovered them in 1980. Sadly, Tovey was to die of a heart attack months after the tour's end.

Depeche largely went to ground in 2002, emerging towards the end of the year to receive an "Innovation Award" from *Q*, one of the many UK music magazines that had spent the last two decades mocking them. A higher form of recognition came when country music icon Johnny Cash chose to cover "Personal Jesus."

Dave Gahan was hugely excited by this. The song's actual author, the reliably underwhelmed Martin Gore, appeared to be less so.

"Martin was all like, 'Yeah, I guess it's pretty good,'" the incredulous Gahan was to report. "I said, 'Martin, this is like Elvis covering one of your songs!'"

Yet the relatively quiet 2002 did not mean that Depeche Mode had been inactive. Tellingly, their two main members had both spent it planning solo albums. Martin Gore was first out of the traps. Recorded at his amusingly nicknamed Electric Ladyboy home studio in Santa Barbara (beneath his shy, silent persona, Gore has always possessed a wicked sense of humor) and released on April 29, 2003, *Counterfeit2* was a fourteen-years-later follow-up to his 1989 *Counterfeit* covers EP.

The album was a collection of sweet, insubstantial synth-driven Gore interpretations of songs as various as David Essex's "Stardust," Brian Eno's "By This River," the blues standard "In My Time of Dying" made famous by both Bob Dylan and Led Zeppelin, and John Lennon's "Oh My Love" ode to Yoko.

Counterfeit2 appeared a pretty but also pretty pointless project, with even Andy Fletcher reportedly finding it "a bit self-indulgent." Critics were not impressed, with the *Guardian*'s Dorian Lynskey nonplussed by Gore's fey mewl through Nick Cave's "Loverman": "Anybody who sounds like Gore should never, ever, not even for a bet, cover a Nick Cave song."

Released a mere six weeks later, Dave Gahan's debut was a different beast entirely. Introduced by

LEFT Johnny Cash covered "Personal Jesus"
CENTRE Martin Gore goes solo in LA, 2003
RIGHT Dave Gahan does the same

a glorious sleazy single, "Dirty Sticky Floors," *Paper Monsters* was a louche swagger of an album that melded glam-rock stomp and electronic textures as well as Depeche ever had. Who knew Gahan had such sharp songwriting chops?

Where *Counterfeit2* had been a commercial flop, *Paper Monsters* was to sneak into the UK Top 40 and yield three Top 40 singles. Gahan also took off on a seventy-date solo world tour that saw him win critical acclaim for his new material. "When Depeche reunite, the balance of power will not be the same," noted the *Independent*.

It was a pertinent point. Gahan had long harbored a quiet wish to contribute songs to Depeche Mode and now, newly cleaned up and focused, he was becoming confident enough to act upon it. Indeed, he had played demos of a couple of his songs to Martin Gore during the *Exciter* sessions, only to receive a typically sphinx-like response.

"He nodded his head and let me know they were pretty good," said Gahan. "But he never turned around and said, 'Great, let's record some for this album.'"

Ever the phlegmatic observer of intra-band tensions, Andy Fletcher reckoned that Gahan had simply chosen the wrong moment to attempt his show-and-tell with Gore.

"David played it wrong," he confided to *Q*. "He played the songs to Martin when he was drunk. Martin made some comments and when he sobered up, he couldn't remember what he'd said."

Gahan's resentment about what he saw as Gore's controlling nature in the studio was laid bare in a series of press interviews to promote *Paper Monsters*. Describing *Exciter* as "Martin's album, but with my voice on it," he told *Rolling Stone* that Depeche Mode simply would not continue unless the band became notably more democratic.

"Unless Martin is open to both me and him coming into the studio with a bunch of songs and supporting each other, I don't see that there's any point in going on and making another Depeche Mode record," he concluded. "You know what? At this point, I just don't care."

Gahan and Gore had agreed that they would speak at the end of 2004, once both their solo projects had

run their course, to discuss what the future held for Depeche Mode. Gore had been hurt by the singer's media broadsides and the first meeting was inevitably a tad frosty. However, peace soon broke out. They found a way forward.

"Dave's songs are really good now," Fletcher reported to Q. "Some of them will earn their place on the album." Having gone into the first meeting demanding the right to write half of the next album, Gahan had happily settled for being allowed to contribute three songs.

Gahan was also more than pleased again to record in Gore's new hometown of Santa Barbara, and the band reconvened in Sound Design studios early in 2005 with a new producer, Ben Hillier, fresh from working with Doves and Blur. The perceptive Hillier intuited what was needed to restore Depeche Mode's mojo.

"*Exciter* was done a lot on laptops—it takes bloody ages and it's very boring for everyone except the person who is actually on the computer," he explained to Steve Malins in *Depeche Mode: A Biography*.

"I wanted to have a live, human, performance element. I like to see a bit of humanism in the music. I think it gives people a way of relating to it and that was the thing I think was missing from the last record."

Hillier was to describe the initial studio atmosphere between Gahan and Gore/Fletcher as "pretty strained" but he soon realized that the newfound rivalry between Gore and Gahan could spur both, and therefore the band, on to greater heights.

"I was concerned that there might be situations where they refused to work on each other's songs," he told Malins. "It could have been disastrous, but they were all great straightaway. They both had the attitude of 'Let's give it a go.'

LEFT A more democratic Depeche Mode
ABOVE In Cologne, Germany, 2005

"There is a competitive streak between Dave and Martin, no doubt about that, but it forced Martin into writing better songs."

As the band grew accustomed to their new dynamic, the album that was to be called *Playing the Angel* came together brilliantly. Gahan was delighted to learn Gore was willing to work his creative magic to embellish the singer's nervously offered contributions.

Gore added plangent guitar chords to the dark throb of Gahan's "I Want It All." He also ladled synth patterns over the brooding "Suffer Well," a song that appeared to find the singer chiding his bandmates for being absent in his drug ravaged hours of need. "Where were you when I fell from grace? A frozen heart, an empty space . . ."

"It was definitely a little dig at them," Gahan was to confirm. "I didn't write it like that, but when I sang it, I did picture Martin. It was, 'Why didn't you understand that I needed you the most then? When I was crawling across the floor of that apartment in Santa Monica, inside I was screaming, 'Where the fuck are you?'"

"There is a competitive streak between Dave and Martin, no doubt about that."

HILLIER

For his part, Gore was coming up with strong songs such as "John the Revelator" and "Lilian" which, in stark contrast to his *Exciter* material, weaved and stung with killer hooks and melodies. He was pouring his heart and soul into the album—maybe as temporary respite from his troubled personal life.

After sixteen years together, that had yielded three children, Gore was going through a painful divorce from his wife, Suzanne Boisvert. He poured the immense guilt he felt about disrupting his kids' lives in this manner into *Playing the Angel*'s standout track, the extremely moving "Precious": "Precious and fragile things/Need special handling/My God, what have we done to you?"

"I feel like I've failed in my marriage," Gore was to confess to *Mojo*. "I feel guilty about that because of the children. Maybe the marriage was partly a charade for a while anyway. I felt guilty about that for . . . I don't know how many years."

A fervent *cri de coeur*, "Precious" was to prove a superb first offering from *Playing the Angel*. Released as the lead single in October 2006, it charted at No. 4 in the UK, a level reached previously only by 1984's "People Are People" and 1997's "Barrel of a Gun." It was a No. 1 in ever-romantic Italy and Spain.

Three weeks later, the vibrant *Playing the Angel* was widely greeted with critical hosannas as an unexpected, but extremely welcome, return to form for Depeche Mode. *Q* magazine led the applause, declaring it to be "the year's greatest and most unlikely comeback."

Veteran critic Andy Gill, writing in the *Independent*, also found much to love. "The band haven't sounded this assured in a while," he wrote, "smoothly slipping from electro-funk to Kraftwerkian grace to a more abstract form of bricolage, sometimes within a single track."

The critics' nods of approval found echoes in the wider world. Outperforming *Exciter* in both countries, *Playing the Angel* charted at No. 6 in the UK and No. 7 in America. The sixteen countries in which it reached No. 1 included France, Germany, Italy, and Portugal.

Nor did Depeche fear touring any longer. With their demons firmly conquered, the *Touring the Angel* jaunt was a joyous affair. Kicking off with a low-key "Starting the Angel" date for competition winners in New York's Bowery Ballroom on October 25, 2005, it lapped the US and Europe twice each, taking in stadium, arena, and festival dates before coming to an end in Athens the following August.

Tellingly, its set list had featured only one song from *Exciter*.

"This tour was probably the most enjoyable, rewarding live show we have ever done," Dave Gahan marveled. "The new material was just waiting to be played live. It took on a life of its own. With the energy of the crowds, it just came to life."

So, Depeche Mode had conquered the world, yet again. Now it was time to train their sights on the universe.

> **"This tour was probably the most enjoyable, rewarding live show we have ever done. The new material was just waiting to be played live. It took on a life of its own."**
>
> **GAHAN**

LEFT No longer fearing touring: Dave Gahan
BELOW Live in LA, December 2005, with Christian Eigner on drums

**"The band haven't sounded
this assured in a while."**

INDEPENDENT

Playing the Angel

TRACK LIST

A Pain That I'm Used To

John The Revelator

Suffer Well

The Sinner In Me

Precious

Macro

I Want It All

Nothing's Impossible

Introspectre

Damaged People

Lilian

The Darkest Star

Recorded at Sound Design, Santa Barbara and Stratosphere Sound, New York, USA, Whitfield Street, London, England

Produced by Ben Hillier & Depeche Mode

Personnel
Dave Gahan
Martin Gore
Andy Fletcher

Cover art
Anton Corbijn

Released 17 Oct 2005

Label Mute CDSTUMM260

Highest chart position on release
UK 6, GER 1, FRA 1, SWE 1, CAN 3, SWI 1, US 7, ITA 1, AUS 45, SPA 2

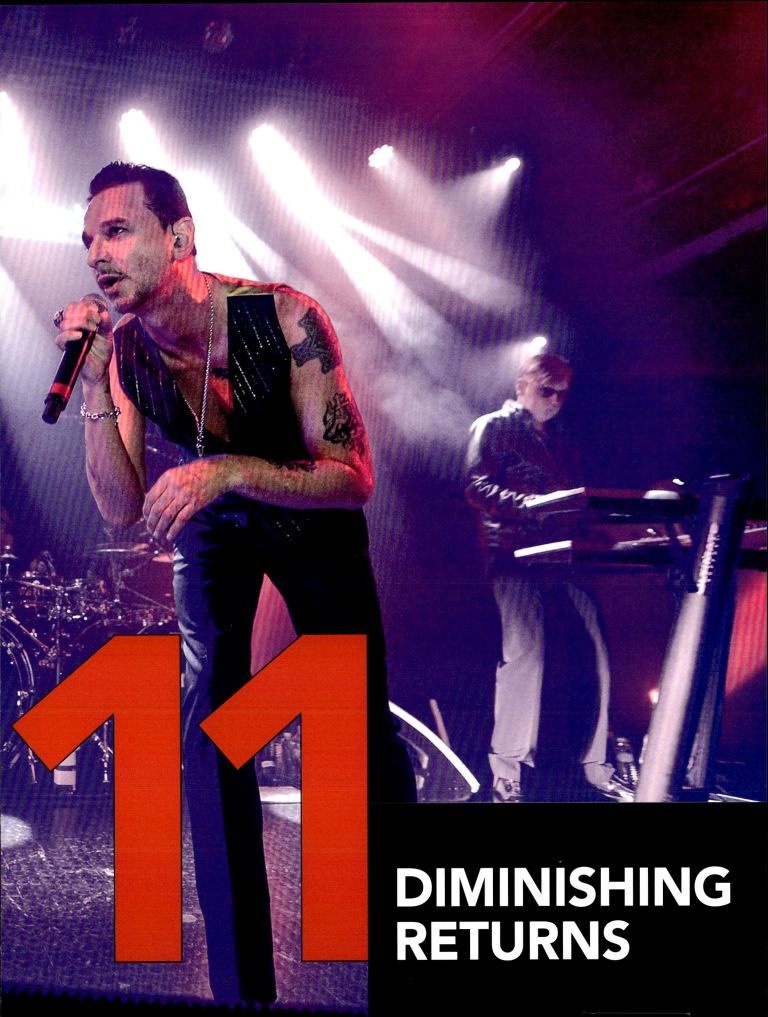

11

DIMINISHING RETURNS

ute Records was no longer what it was. The punky cottage-industry label that Daniel Miller had launched nearly forty years earlier had over the years become a major independent music player—but it had also had to alter its setup to adapt to changing times.

With digital piracy and falling CD sales eating into record company bottom lines, Miller had admitted that in the late nineties the label was facing financial problems. Luckily the prodigious sales of Moby's *Play* album, together with the continued success of Depeche Mode, Erasure, and Nick Cave, had helped to steady the ship.

However, like many other independent UK labels, including Rough Trade and Creation, Mute had linked up with a major. In 2002, EMI had bought the company for £23 million, although Miller continued to run it as company chairman and claimed to have an "astonishing" degree of autonomy.

Whether the impetus was coming from Miller or his new corporate paymasters, Mute appeared to have a new focus on maximizing and monetizing Depeche Mode's back catalog. After a *Remixes 81–04* remix album in 2004, 2006 was to see both a 644-track *The Complete Depeche Mode* download-only album and a more conventional CD compilation, *The Best of Depeche Mode Volume 1*.

Needing a new single to promote this latter set, Depeche returned to a song which they had worked on in Santa Barbara but which failed to make the cut for *Playing the Angel*. Originally called "Martyr for Love," "Martyr" wrapped a typical anguished Gore musing on the pain of infatuation in an upbeat, radio-friendly electro-coating.

The strategy worked. "Martyr" charted at a respectable No. 13 in the UK—and was a No. 1 in Italy and Spain—while *The Best of Depeche Mode* was to sell a million copies in Europe, powered by its strong performance in ever-loyal Germany, where it reached No. 2.

After the success of *Paper Monsters*, EMI were also keen to promote Dave Gahan as a solo artist and in 2007 he released his second solo album, *Hourglass*. Of a less rock and roll, more electronic bent than his

debut, it was again a minor critical and commercial success, but Gahan decided against touring it.

This was largely because Depeche Mode were about to spring back into album action.

Reuniting with producer Ben Hillier in Santa Barbara, in May 2008 the band began work on the album that was to become *Sounds of the Universe*. The sessions would certainly be the most sober the band had ever been involved with: having decided that his own drinking was problematic, Martin Gore had joined Gahan in turning teetotal.

Indeed, Gahan was to report that the recording process proved to be unusually businesslike.

"In the context of our output, this is probably one of the most disciplined records we've made," he told music

PREVIOUS PAGE KROQ presents Depeche Mode at The Troubadour, West Hollywood

LEFT Dave Gahan off stage

RIGHT Daniel Miller sold Mute Records to EMI for £23m

"It's hard not to feel disappointed by the sense that a band who have raised their game so many times have nowhere new to go."

Q MAGAZINE

BELOW Three different images in one band, 2009
RIGHT "It's a larf, innit?" *The Tour of the Universe* reaches London's O2 Arena

website *The Quietus.* "Martin and I just turned up every day to work, both of us very focussed. He's written some fantastic songs, and I've got a few on there, myself.

"We've made records with all kinds of different stuff going on. People leaving the band, personal stuff going on—and sometimes you get to the end of a record and you're glad it's finished. But there was something different about this one . . ."

Gahan made the album's recording sound a slick, unchallenging process—and when *Sounds of the Universe* appeared, on April 17, 2009, that was exactly what it sounded like. By now Depeche Mode could produce this kind of sleek, pulsing electro-goth in their sleep, and it appeared that that was what they were doing.

The album had one undoubted, mesmerizing peak—the pulverizing "Wrong," its insistent throb reminiscent of "Personal Jesus," in which, courtesy of Gore's words, Gahan appeared to speculate that he had been destined to live his life lived wildly and none too wisely: "I was born in the wrong sign/In the wrong house/With the wrong ascendancy/I took the wrong road . . ." A shoo-in for the album's lead-off single, it faltered in the UK due to little radio play, but hit No. 1 in Italy.

Elsewhere, though, *Sounds of the Universe* sounded a tad too much like Depeche Mode going through the motions. "In Chains" and the Gahan-penned "Hole to Feed" had a certain élan but the quality fell away precipitously in the second half of the record, with the nadir being anonymous instrumental "Spacewalker."

A few critics lauded a perceived newfound "maturity" on the album (often a dread word when applied to pop music) but others railed at its predictableness. *Rolling Stone* thought it "a time machine back to the Eighties" while Jon Pareles in the *New York Times* felt it to be "seamless Depeche Mode filler, music that could be made by any number of acolytes."

However, it was a long-time band supporter, the reliably perceptive Dorian Lynskey, who most succinctly identified *Sounds of the Universe*'s limitations in a review in *Q* magazine:

> At the 12th time of asking, to play the fan-pleasing goth-pop card, or to attempt something more testing? Alas, once again, it's the former . . .
>
> Their 12th album feels like being at the heart of a magnificent but slow-moving machine, shaded midnight blue and battleship grey. The synths are dense and enveloping, and Gahan's voice becomes ever richer with age—everything sounds right, but too few of the songs stick . . .

It's hard not to feel disappointed by the sense that a band who have raised their game so many times have nowhere new to go . . . as Gahan croons on one of his three compositions, "Miles Away/The Truth Is," "It's one of those conversations, we've had them before."

These shortcomings did not prevent *Sounds of the Universe* charting high. A No. 1 in sixteen countries, from Mexico to Russia, it reached No. 2 in the UK, kept off the top only by Lady Gaga's *The Fame*, and No. 3 in the US, the band's highest placing since *Songs of Faith and Devotion*.

However, it was notable in most major territories that sales fell away very quickly after the first week, with devoted fans snapping up the record on release but few more casual purchasers being tempted. Maybe Depeche Mode were returning to being that cult band again.

"The synths are dense and enveloping, and Gahan's voice becomes ever richer with age—everything sounds right, but too few of the songs stick."

Q

Sounds of the Universe

TRACK LIST

In Chains
Hole to Feed
Wrong
Fragile Tension
Little Soul
In Sympathy
Peace

Come Back
Spacewalker
Perfect
Miles Away / The Truth Is
Jezebel
Corrupt
Wrong [Reprise] (hidden track)

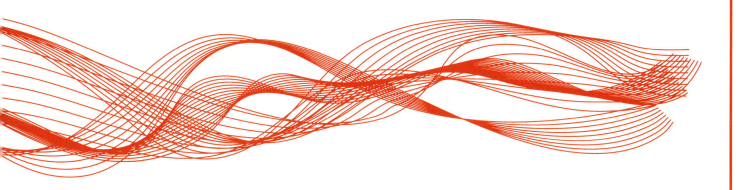

Recorded at Chung King Studios, New York and Sound Design, Santa Barbara, USA

Produced by Ben Hillier & Depeche Mode

Personnel
Dave Gahan
Martin Gore
Andy Fletcher

Cover art
Anton Corbijn

Released 17 Apr 2009

Label Mute CDSTUMM300

Highest chart position on release
UK 2, GER 1, FRA 2, SWE 1, CAN 3, SWI 1, US 3, ITA 1, AUS 32, SPA 1

The group immediately began gearing up for the mammoth *Tour of the Universe* to promote the album. This was a jaunt on which the man formerly known as "The Cat" used up a few more lives.

After a warm-up show rather quaintly held in Luxembourg on May 6, Depeche visited Israel for the first time. They then looked to begin a run of European dates—at which point, disaster struck.

Waiting to take the stage before the show, in Athens on May 12, Dave Gahan was taken ill and rushed to hospital. Gastroenteritis was initially diagnosed, but further tests revealed that he had developed a malignant, cancerous tumor in his bladder.

A month's worth of dates were rescheduled or cancelled as Gahan was successfully operated on and then recuperated. The tour picked up again in Germany in early June, but a month later the front man pulled a calf muscle onstage at the BBK Live festival in Bilbao, Spain, leading to two more dates being nixed.

Gahan had recovered by the time the North American leg of the tour kicked off in Toronto on July 24, but just two weeks later he strained his vocal cords during a show at Seattle's Key Arena. Two more dates bit the dust as the unlucky singer's voice healed.

Yet despite these mishaps, *Tour of the Universe* was a major success, packing out multiple nights at New York's Madison Square Garden, L.A.'s Hollywood Bowl, and London's O2 arena. When Depeche Mode played a Teenage Cancer Trust show at London's Royal Albert Hall on February 10, Alan Wilder made a nostalgic slight return, playing piano on "Somebody" from *Some Great Reward*. By the time the tour closed in Dusseldorf, two weeks later, it had grossed close to £170 million.

It was now time for Depeche Mode to head off and work on separate projects again: maybe that was how they now kept some perspective and their sanity. Dave Gahan had grown close to Soulsavers, a UK dance/production duo who had supported Depeche on some *Tour of the Universe* European dates, and recorded an excellent album with them, *The Light the Dead See*.

Five years after his divorce from Suzanne, Martin Gore's personal life took a fresh twist as he met and began dating an English actress now living in the US, the thirty-year-old Kerrilee Kaski. His next musical side-project was highly unexpected: he got back together with Vince Clarke.

With the resentment at Clarke's abrupt departure from Depeche Mode thirty years earlier long gone, Gore was delighted when his former bandmate

asked him to collaborate on a one-off album of electro-instrumentals. It was an utterly unexpected invitation, but also a welcome one—maybe, even, providing some closure?

Adopting the spectacularly uninventive band name VCMG, the pair got together to record an album of exquisite techno-doodles. Or, rather, they didn't, working remotely from separate continents via file-sharing. The resulting record, *Ssss*, sounded sweet, slightly dated, and received little attention except, inevitably, in Germany.

Depeche Mode now seemed to have fallen into a rather comfortable work routine. They put out an album every four years, bought by the faithful but few new converts, then schlepped it round the world's enormo-domes for a year or more. It was a convenient routine—and a highly lucrative one.

Thus, the band reconvened in early spring 2012, once again in Santa Barbara, once again with producer Ben Hillier. The thinking seemed to be if it ain't broke, don't fix it—but when *Delta Machine* emerged, in March 2013, it was clear that this routine was patently producing routine albums.

Like *Playing the Angel*, like *Sounds of the Universe*, *Delta Machine* wasn't a dreadful Depeche Mode

"**The partnership of the singer David Gahan and songwriter Martin Gore can't escape the machine they've become, or the holding pattern they're stuck in.**"

PITCHFORK

Tour of the Universe hits Berlin (left) and Miami (right)

Depeche Mode: the venues just keep getting bigger

album. It was . . . just another Depeche Mode album. All of their tics, trademarks, and defining ideas and sounds were present and correct, but it was hard to escape the feeling you had heard it all before.

The first single, the pensive electro-ballad "Heaven," was well worked, but could have been from any album from *Violator* onwards. Gahan was in fine, redolent voice on "Secret to the End" and his own "Should Be Higher" but, again, it was hard to escape the stifling sense of déjà vu.

As usual, some reviews praised *Delta Machine*'s textures and clever craftsmanship, but others mourned the album's lack of cutting edge and apparent complacency. Where was the drive, the passion, the originality, the soul? Where was the longing to invent the future?

Hipster music website *Pitchfork* put the boot in the most forensically. Noting that the record sounded like a set of outtakes from *Songs of Faith and Devotion*, a record released twenty years earlier, their critic, Douglas Wolk, accused the band, once pioneers, of resting firmly on their laurels:

> People who make machines use the term "delta" to mean "change." Depeche Mode aren't so keen on that any more . . .
>
> The partnership of the singer David Gahan and songwriter Martin Gore can't escape the machine they've become, or the holding pattern they're stuck in (and then there's third member, Andy Fletcher, who . . . anyway!) . . .
>
> What made Depeche Mode work, when they worked, wasn't just the contrast between Gore's dry detachment and Gahan's dorky innocence . . . It was their constant pushing forward of their sound—expanding the vocabulary of what electronics could do in pop songs . . .
>
> But they stopped pushing forward long ago, and now they don't even bother pretending technology has opened up any possibilities for recorded sound in the last twenty years . . .
>
> There is not a single moment of shock or freshness on *Delta Machine*, and it's enormously frustrating to hear what was once a band of futurists so deeply mired in resisting change.

It was hard to quibble with a word of this critique. The album did as well as twenty-first-century

Depeche Mode albums invariably do, reaching No. 2 in the UK and topping the chart in more than twenty countries, including Germany and Italy. It even went platinum in France.

The subsequent 107-date *Delta Machine Tour* also cleaned up as per usual, grossing close on £200 million as it shoehorned more than two million people into the world's arenas over its ten-month run. It even ventured to pastures new—Belarus and Abu Dhabi—before climaxing with a March 7 show at the Olympic Stadium in Moscow.

Once quirky electro-punks, then raging out-of-control party animals, Depeche Mode had now seemingly morphed, both on record and on the road, into a slick, clinical world-domination musical

machine, an object lesson in giving the devoted exactly what they wanted and not fucking with the formula. Their fire, their creative fervency, looked to be fully extinguished and unlikely ever to be lit again.

Which made what happened next all the more extraordinary.

Gore and Fletcher (left) and Gahan (right):
"a slick, clinical, world-domination musical machine"

"They stopped pushing forward long ago, and now they don't even bother pretending technology has opened up any possibilities."

PITCHFORK

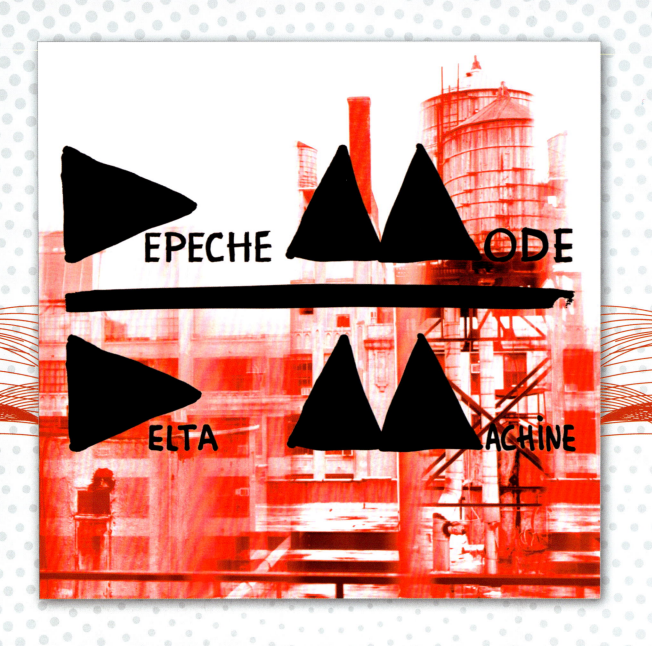

"There is not a single moment of shock or freshness on *Delta Machine*, and it's enormously frustrating."

PITCHFORK

Delta Machine

TRACK LIST

Welcome to My World

Angel

Heaven

Secret to The End

My Little Universe

Slow

Broken

The Child Inside

Soft Touch/Raw Nerve

Should Be Higher

Alone

Soothe My Soul

Goodbye

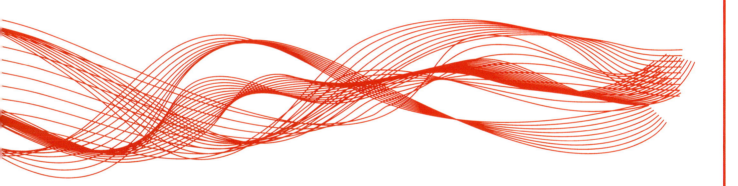

Recorded at Jungle City Studios, New York and Sound Design, Santa Barbara, USA

Produced by Ben Hillier & Depeche Mode

Personnel
Dave Gahan
Martin Gore
Andy Fletcher

Cover art
Anton Corbijn

Released 22 Mar 2013

Label Mute 88765460622

Highest chart position on release
UK 2, GER 1, FRA 2, SWE 1, CAN 2, SWI 1, US 6, ITA 1, AUS 16, SPA 2

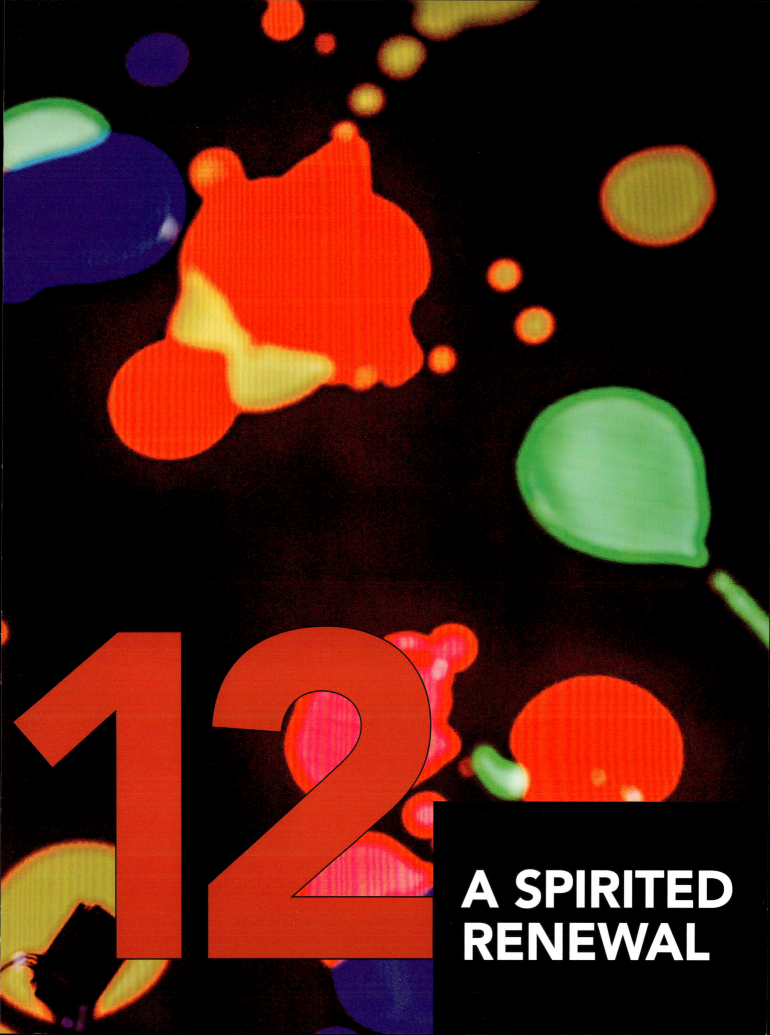

12

A SPIRITED
RENEWAL

Depeche Mode had never been a political band. Dissuaded, maybe, by the affectionate mockery that had greeted cack-handed early forays into social comment such as "Everything Counts" and "People Are People," they had long steered clear of societal analysis. As Dave Gahan had said, as long ago as *Construction Time Again*: "We don't have political views, I don't think."

In addition, as the second decade of the twenty-first century neared its halfway point, they had no reason to take issue with the world. Their own personal lives were uncharacteristically settled. The now-sober Gahan had found happiness in New York with his wife, Jennifer; married more than twenty years, Andy Fletcher remained a contented family man.

Three months after the *Delta Machine Tour* ended, Martin Gore completed the trio of domestic bliss by marrying his girlfriend of three years, Kerrilee Kaski, on June 12 in the Turks and Caicos Islands. He spent the next year pottering and recording an album of sixteen electronic instrumentals, *MG*, in his Electric Ladyboy home studio. On February 19, 2016, Kaski gave birth to a baby daughter, Johnnie Lee.

All was rosy in Depeche Mode's world . . . but as the band began to contemplate beginning work on their next album it was clear that in the wider world, something profoundly malign was afoot.

Around the US and Western Europe, the liberal and social democratic consensus that had mostly governed progressively for decades had been broken. An ugly new mood of populism was emerging, with racism, intolerance, and fear of immigration on the rise.

In the UK, then-Prime Minister David Cameron attempted to mollify right-wing elements in his governing Conservative Party by calling a referendum on Britain's continued membership of the European Union. He was convinced he would win: the leaders

PREVIOUS PAGE Olympic Stadium, Rome, 2017

LEFT Striking a pose, Arena Birmingham, UK

BELOW Martin Gore and star guitar, Oracle Arena, Oakland, California

"**The world is in a big mess at the moment. And it is very difficult, I think, to make an album and not acknowledge that.**"

GAHAN

of a series of mass rallies at which his dog-whistle speeches pandered to disaffected Middle America's worst instincts. He threatened to renegotiate all existing US trade deals; clamp down on immigration to America, particularly targeting Muslim would-be immigrants; and build a giant wall along the US's southern border to keep out Mexican "drug dealers, criminals and rapists."

Accused of various sexual assaults in his past, Trump was caught on tape speaking of his fondness for grabbing women "by the pussy." In a CNN TV interview, he even declined to condemn the Klu Klux Klan. Despite all this, he and Democratic candidate Hillary Clinton were running neck and neck.

Such was the mood music, then, when Depeche Mode gathered in Santa Barbara in April 2016 to record their fourteenth studio album. Having decided that, after three albums, their relationship with Ben Hillier had become a little too cozy, they had opted for a new producer in Simian Mobile Disco member and Arctic Monkeys producer James Ford.

The recording of the album, *Spirit*, was to take four months, split as usual between Santa Barbara and Jungle Studios in New York, and it was clear that while they were working, Depeche Mode were paying close attention to the collapse of the liberal world around them. For any sentient being, it was impossible not to.

Martin Gore confirmed the focus of the album at a press event in Milan on October 11, 2016, after the recording had been completed.

"The world is in a big mess at the moment," he said. "And it is very difficult, I think, to make an album and not acknowledge that—to brush it all aside and pretend it's not happening."

For his part, the usually apolitical Dave Gahan expressed alarm at the rise of Trump, and at his toxic rhetoric at his campaign rallies.

"The things that he's saying sound very similar to what someone was saying in 1935," he stated, referencing the rise of Hitler in Germany's Weimar Republic. "That didn't work out very well. The things that he [Trump] is saying are cruel and heartless and promoting fear."

Less than a month later, on November 8, 2016, Donald J. Trump was elected the forty-fifth president of the United States.

One factor in Trump's rise had been the coagulation around him, and support for him, of a faction known as the alternative right, or "alt-right,"

of all three major British political parties were urging people to vote to remain in the EU, as were business and union leaders.

Cameron miscalculated badly. Seduced by charismatic but seemingly fork-tongued figures such as United Kingdom Independence Party (UKIP) leader Nigel Farage and rogue Tory Minister Boris Johnson, on June 23, 2016, the British people voted to leave the European Union they had belonged to for more than forty years. The wheels of Brexit were set in motion.

Like millions more, Depeche Mode were dumbfounded by this development.

"I was shocked," Dave Gahan was to admit. "I've lived in America for 25 years but I didn't really think that many people would vote to leave the EU. I think most people didn't really understand what that meant. They were not well informed."

"We're all depressed by the outcome of the referendum," added Martin Gore. "I think it was a really stupid idea to leave something so important to the people, because even top financial people don't understand what the impact of that [Brexit] is going to be."

Meanwhile, over in America, something even more damaging for world peace and prosperity was brewing. Motivated seemingly by little more than a visceral hatred for sitting US President Barack Obama, a New York property tycoon and former reality TV show star, Donald Trump, had been voted the Republican Party's Presidential candidate.

Running under the slogan of "Make America Great Again," Trump's campaign largely consisted a grouping of far-right ideologues whose wild outer reaches housed white supremacists and neo-fascists. Bizarrely, Depeche Mode were about to be pulled into this group's poisoned orbit.

Richard B. Spencer, a white nationalist who headed up an extremist think tank called the National Policy Institute and who claimed to have coined the term "alt-right," attended Trump's inauguration in Washington, D.C. on January 20, 2017. While being interviewed by a TV crew in the street, he was punched in the head by a masked protestor.

The next month, before being kicked out of the Conservative Political Action Conference, near Washington, for his "repugnant" views, Spencer was asked by New York magazine whether he liked rock music. He replied: "Depeche Mode is the official band of the alt-right."

Spencer later claimed on Twitter that he was "joking" but added that he was "a lifelong Depeche Mode fan." Speaking to Rolling Stone, he outlined the twisted appeal he had somehow located in the band.

"They aren't a typical rock band, in terms of lyrics and much else," he said. "Depeche Mode is a band of existential angst, pain, sadism, horror, darkness and much more . . .

"There was a certain Communist aesthetic to an early album like A Broken Frame as well as titles like Music for the Masses but then there's a bit of a fascist element, too. It's obviously ambiguous and, as with all art, everything is multilayer, contradictory and ambivalent."

This was not an endorsement that any sane band would want to pick up and a horrified Depeche Mode quickly issued a press statement dismissing Spencer's attempted co-opting of them as "ridiculous." "Depeche Mode has no ties to Richard Spencer or the alt-right and does not support the alt-right movement," they added.

Richard B. Spencer (center): "Depeche Mode is the official band of the alt-right."

> ## "Depeche Mode are growing old angrily, and it suits them."
>
> **CLASSIC ROCK**

Together, forever: Gore and Gahan in Prague

Media interviews timed around the release of *Spirit* on March 17, 2017 gave the group a chance to develop this theme and Dave Gahan, in particular, did not hold back. Asked about Spencer by the *New York Post*, he told them: "I saw the video of him getting punched. He deserved it!"

Speaking to US entertainment industry bible *Billboard*, Gahan was even less equivocal, falling back into the vernacular of a Basildon saloon bar.

"What's dangerous about someone like Richard Spencer is, first of all, he's a cunt," he explained. "And he's a very educated cunt, and that's the scariest kind of all.

"I think over the years there have been a number of times when things of ours have been misinterpreted—either our imagery, or something where people are not quite reading between the lines."

Gahan had also made another, very apposite remark that hinted at the content and direction of Depeche Mode's imminent album.

"It really is about the condition [of the world]," he said. "I think the album provokes and pushes for you, the listener, as well to question your condition and the way you think, and [ask], 'What are we heading for? What have we achieved here?'"

It was Dave Gahan's job to talk up Depeche Mode's new album as a provocative, questioning response to global politics' new mood of brutalism. Yet when *Spirit* finally appeared, it was immediately clear that his rhetoric was entirely justified.

The tone was set by the album's itchy, querulous opening track. Over a twitchy, glitchy beat, "Going Backwards" found Gahan bemoaning a world in which human evolution had been reversed: "We're going backwards/Turning back our history . . . piling on the misery."

Next up, the album's lead single, "Where's the Revolution," cut to the chase even more dramatically. Over fluttering electronics—and Ford and his production sidekick on Spirit, Matrixxman, were certainly finding sonic angles and textures sorely missing from the last few Depeche albums—Gahan's rich brown croon listed the ways people had been lied to and deceived in the grim new Trump/Brexit era.

"You've been kept down . . . pushed 'round . . . pissed on for too long . . ." he exhorted, before building to the song's demagogic, truly rousing chorus: "Where's the revolution/Come on, people/ You're letting me down!" Even imagining the lines being sung en masse by twenty thousand Depeche followers in the world's arenas excited goose bumps.

And so it went on. "The Worst Crime" began with a depiction of a public lynching and harangued the huddled masses for allowing the rise of political evil through their "apathetic hesitation." The dark-eyed, vengeful "Scum" grabbed Trump and his henchmen by the lapels and shook them, demanding to know what they would do ". . . when karma comes."

Elsewhere on the album, the moody, brooding Gahan-penned "Poison Heart" could equally easily have been applied to his venal, opportunistic former L.A. drug buddies or to the current, morally bankrupt leaders of the free world. "You know it's time to break up," he drawled at his unidentified nemesis. "You'll always be alone."

"Poorman" came surprisingly close to being "Everything Counts" redux as Gore's lyric depicted the pitiful lot of a homeless drifter before concluding, "Corporations get the breaks/Keeping almost everything they make." Slipping sarcastically into the language of the Adam Smith Institute, he rhetorically inquired: "When will it trickle down?"

Spirit was patently Depeche Mode's twenty-first-century electro-industrial take on *What's Going On* and it reached its apogee in the closing none-more-bleak techno-ballad "Fail." Over alternately clanking and chiming beats, Martin Gore crooned the grimmest of conclusions on humanity's current state of play: "Oh, we're fucked."

Well, who had seen this one coming? Where they had appeared to be aimlessly drifting on their last three albums, Depeche Mode had snapped back into focus and produced a coruscating, powerful sociopolitical statement. Talking to *loudandquiet. com* on *Spirit*'s release, Dave Gahan rammed the point home:

> *Spirit* is more of a social outlook on humanity itself, and we're lost. We seem to be pretending we're not but we're fucking lost!
>
> Where's the spirit? Where's the spirit in really caring? People say, "It's easy for you guys in your fancy houses" but, like Martin has said, just because you've had some success it doesn't mean you have to stop caring about what you see and feel.
>
> You do the best you can. The way we can portray how we feel is through music, through art. Ultimately, we're here to entertain you— but to maybe entertain you with a sense of reflecting.

Critics who had grown accustomed to giving Depeche Mode albums three stars out of five and declaring them to be more of the same old same old reacted delightedly to *Spirit*'s venom and sense of purpose. "It's easy to get swept away in their gospel," nodded *Rolling Stone*, while *Classic Rock* noted, "Depeche Mode are growing old angrily, and it suits them."

Writing in the *Guardian*, Alexis Petridis had high praise for Depeche's new charged, visceral ire. They were, he acknowledged, a band reborn.

"Depeche Mode have released an album that gives every impression of being an hour-long howl of outrage and horror at a world in which people such as Richard Spencer appear to be in the ascendant . . ." he wrote, concluding: "Depeche Mode sound raw and alive and rigidly opposed to merely going through the motions."

"Depeche Mode sound raw
and alive and rigidly opposed to
merely going through the motions."

GUARDIAN

Spirit

TRACK LIST

Going Backwards

Where's the Revolution

The Worst Crime

Scum

You Move

Cover Me

Eternal

Poison Heart

So Much Love

Poorman

No More (This Is the Last Time)

Fail

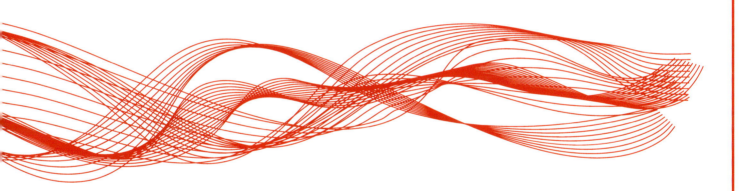

Recorded at Jungle City Studios, New York and Sound Design, Santa Barbara, USA

Produced by James Ford & Depeche Mode

Personnel
Dave Gahan
Martin Gore
Andy Fletcher

Cover art
Anton Corbijn

Released 17 Mar 2017

Label Mute 88985411651

Highest chart position on release
UK 5, GER 1, FRA 1, SWE 3, CAN 4, SWI 1,
US 5, ITA 1, AUS 14, SPA 2

"**Depeche Mode have released an album that gives every impression of being an hour-long howl of outrage and horror.**"

GUARDIAN

From the vivid stabs of the beats to the impassioned imprecations of the lyrics and their energized explanations of *Spirit* to the media, it was palpable that Depeche Mode believed more deeply in their fourteenth studio album than they had in any for years. This faith in their new child, this devotion, was rewarded when it hit No. 1 in a whole slew of countries, and reached No. 5 in both the UK and the US.

The world clearly liked *Spirit* and Depeche Mode were determined to take it to them. Two months later, they began the biggest global tour they had ever played.

Starting in Stockholm on May 5, the *Global Spirit* odyssey criss-crossed the planet, over six legs, for fourteen months, grossing more than £250 million from its 130 shows. By the time it climaxed with two nights back at the Waldbühne in Berlin on July 23 and 25, 2018, it had entertained more than two-and-a-half million people. Maybe the revolution was right there, all the time.

Sometimes, stories turn full circle. When Depeche Mode closed the *Global Spirit* tour at the Waldbühne in July 2018, their support came from Deutsch Amerikanische Freundschaft, or DAF—one of the first two acts Daniel Miller had released on Mute Records, forty years earlier. One can only imagine the conversations backstage.

Depeche Mode themselves celebrate their fortieth anniversary next year and it will naturally be a time for nostalgia and reflection. They may try to swerve the

Launching the *Global Spirit* tour on October 11, 2016 in Milan nostalgic celebrations—futurists tend not to be big on them—but it would be hard for Martin Gore, Andy Fletcher, and Dave Gahan not to reflect on the road they have traveled.

One main conclusion they may reach is that they are lucky still to be here at all. There have been many occasions when they might easily have thrown in the towel, from Vince Clarke's abrupt departure in 1981 to Fletcher's on-the-road 1990s breakdowns. Most of all, when Dave "The Cat" Gahan was using up the last of his nine lives in an L.A. hotel in 1996, it seemed impossible he would be hale, hearty, and thriving more than twenty years later.

Depeche Mode have quite the story, quite the career, to look back on—and they can do so with pride. Few bands of their generation survive. Of those that do, most, such as The Cure or New Order, are in semi-retirement, emerging occasionally to top up the pension fund via lucrative play-the-hits arena tours and festival headline sets.

Depeche Mode have, over the years, had their own spells of resting on their laurels, of creative ennui or inertia, yet, somehow, they have kept the knack of snapping out of them, of spearing the malaise, of becoming fresh, relevant, and vital once more. The baleful *Spirit* made clear that they still have restless souls, questing minds . . . and the knack for pop tunes that so amazed Daniel Miller at the Canning Town Bridge House, all those years ago.

They started out making machine music, yet as they grew up in the public eye they proved themselves to be vulnerably human. However, even if Depeche Mode allow themselves a nostalgic reverie, or even a big fortieth anniversary commemorative tour, they will still have one curious eye fixed firmly on the future.

These outsider artists, these most unlikely pop stars, have come a long, long way from boring Basildon. It would be a foolish man indeed who hazarded a bet that their extraordinary story is anywhere near being over.

It ends here: the *Global Spirit* tour climaxes in the Waldbühne, Berlin, July 2018

Acknowledgments, Sources, Picture Credits

ACKNOWLEDGMENTS

I first realised how globally massive Depeche Mode are when I was living in Siberia in 1993. They were turbulent times in Russia, and one day I went to Red Square in Moscow to find three unofficial parades marching around the square: anti-Boris Yeltsin agitators, pro-Yeltsin supporters, and a peroxided, bullet-belt-wearing army of Depeche Mode fans celebrating Dave Gahan's birthday.

The Mode have only got bigger since, and I have enjoyed writing this book and chronicling their inexorable rise. I would like to thank Mick Paterson for his accounts of wanting to punch music journalists' fucking lights out, and Miles Goosens for sharing his tale of an extraordinary encounter in the Appalachian Mountains. I would like to almost thank Doug McCarthy and Steev Toth – you meant well, and at least we had a pint and a catch-up, Steev. Heartfelt thanks to my editor, Rob Nichols, for being flexible on deadlines when Sir Billy Connolly rather unexpectedly entered my life, and to Gill Woolcott for making sure that not too many of this book's pages are upside-down. Hopefully.

I'd also like to thank Martin Gore, Andrew Fletcher and Alan Wilder for that entertaining early-hours 1994 encounter in a Somerset B&B, when they let me be their moral budgie. You guys are certainly not brain-affected.

Faith and Devotion is for my fellow budgie on that strange night: Phil Nicholls.

SOURCES

Magazines and newspapers: *NME, Melody Maker, Sounds, Uncut, Q, Mojo, The Independent, No 1, New Sounds New Styles, Record Mirror, Smash Hits, Sound On Sound, Daily Star, Daily Telegraph, Daily Mirror, The Times, New York Times, Select, Trouser Press, Rolling Stone, Kingsize, ZigZag, Vox, International Musician and Recording World, The Observer, The Guardian, Los Angeles Times, MT, The Face, Spin, New York Post, Billboard, New York, Classic Rock.*

TV, Radio, Websites and Films: *Synth Britannia, Top of the Pops* (both BBC)*, MTV, Recoil* (recoil.co.uk)*, Depeche Mode* (depechemode.com)*, 101, Reading Pronunciation* (readingpronunciation.blogspot.com)*, Loud and Quiet* (loudandquiet.com)*, Pitchfork* (pitchfork.com)*, KROQ, The Quietus* (thequietus.com)*, Twitter, CNN, Fox News.*

Books

Baker, Trevor, *Depeche Mode: The Early Years*: Independent Music Press, 2013

Malins, Steve, *Depeche Mode: A Biography*: Andre Deutsch, 1999

Miller, Jonathan, *Stripped: Depeche Mode*: Omnibus Press, 2003

Reynolds, Simon, *Rip It Up And Start Again: Postpunk 1978-1984*: Faber & Faber, 2006

Sixx, Nikki and Gittins, Ian, *The Heroin Diaries: A Year in the Life of a Shattered Rock Star*: Pocket Books, 2007

Stubbs, David, *Mars By 1980: The Story of Electronic Music*: Faber & Faber, 2018

Author's interview with Mick Paterson.

PICTURE CREDITS

Courtesy of Alamy AF archive: 70; Anthony Pidgeon/MediaPunch: 174; dpa picture alliance: 68, 76, 77, 78, 87, 92, 94t, 94b, 133, 141, 206; Everett Collection Inc: 16; Igor Vidyashev/ZUMAPRESS.com: 8; John Bentley: 22; LFI/Photoshot: 67; MPVCVRART: 17; Oleg Konin: 104; Pictorial Press Ltd: 14, 19, 25, 86, 90, 101, 132; Roman Vondrous/CTK Photo: 232; Soeren Stache/dpa: 239; Stephen Wood/Pictorial Press Ltd: 58; The Photo Access: 229; Trinity Mirror/Mirrorpix: 12, 18, 24r; WENN Rights Ltd: 214; Zoonar GmbH: 231; ZUMA Press Inc: 221b

Courtesy of Avalon C.L. Kirsch/Retna UK/Photoshot: 138; LFI/Photoshot: 24l, 61, 66l, 66t, 66b, 83, 202r; Michael Putland/Retna UK/Photoshot: 39; Picture Alliance/Avalon. red: 84; PYMCA/Photoshot: 82, 181; Retna/Photoshot: 23, 88, 89, 91, 95t, 117, 120, 126, 127, 131, 134, 189t, 203, 212; Spiros Politis/Retna Pictures/Photoshot: 4; Steve Currid/Retna Pictures/Photoshot: 2

Courtesy of Getty Al Pereira/Michael Ochs Archives: 139; Alison Braun/Michael Ochs Archives: 157; Allan Tannenbaum: 54; Andreas Rentz: 222; Anthony Pidgeon/Redferns: 150; Brian Rasic: 177, 192; Dave Hogan/Hulton Archive: 26t; David Corio/Michael Ochs Archives: 20, 27, 28, 32, 38; David Corio/Redferns: 47; David Redfern/Redferns: 95b, 125; Ebet Roberts/Redferns: 56, 106; FG/Bauer-Griffin: 52, 59; Fin Costello/Redferns: 6, 49; Frank Lennon/Toronto Star: 102; Franziska Krug: 189b; GARCIA/Gamma-Rapho: 142, 164tl; Gie Knaeps: 74; Gina Ferazzi/Los Angeles Times: 154; Harry Langdon: 202l; Jakubaszek: 218, 220, 221t; Jason Merritt for Press Here: 201; Jazz Archiv Hamburg/ullstein bild: 110, 111, 114, 115, 140; Jim Dyson: 197, 215; Joe Dilworth/Photoshot: 193, 205; John Shearer/WireImage: 223; Karl Walter: 207; Koh Hasebe/Shinko Music: 107, 148; Lisa Haun/Michael Ochs Archives: 15, 55; Michael Putland: 43, 73, 93; Michel Delsol: 35; Mick Hutson/Redferns: 163, 164b, 165, 171; Peter Noble/Redferns: 50, 57; Peter Still/Redferns: 156, 164tr, 169; Philip Ramey/Corbis via Getty Images: 219; Rob Verhorst/Redferns: 64, 112, 136, 144, 152; Roberto Panucci /Corbis: 226; Rune Hellestad/CORBIS: 124; Sam Thomas/Gamma-Rapho: 200; SGranitz/WireImage: 177; Sony Music Archive/Mark Baker: 155; Steve Eichner: 153; Tim Mosenfelder: 190; Virginia Turbett/Redferns: 30, 36, 40; Vittorio Zunino Celotto: 236

Courtesy of Rex/Shutterstock Andre Csillag: 41, 46; Anthony Pidgeon/Mediapunch: 159, 167; Chris Pizzello/AP: 188; Eugene Adebari: 130; Gunter W Kienitz: 71; Ian Dickson: 168; Ilpo Musto: 10, 26b, 65; ITV: 97, 166; Jason Sheldon: 228; Joseph Branston/Future Publishing: 213; Nick Ut/AP: 184; Piers Allardyce: 178; REX/Shutterstock: 123, 172; Sunshine International: 33, 75, 79; Unimedia: cover image